BETTER THAN THE BINGE

BETTER THAN THE BINGE

OVERCOMING THE SOCIAL OBLIGATION OF ALCOHOL

ADAM S. LAMB

LIONCREST
PUBLISHING

BETTER THAN THE BINGE
Overcoming the Social Obligation of Alcohol

ISBN   978-1-61961-687-5 *Paperback*
        978-1-61961-688-2 *Ebook*

CONTENTS

INTRODUCTION

When you quit drinking, people tend to assume the worst. They think surely you must have received a DUI, crashed your car, or screamed obscenities at your wife. Who can blame them? Most of the time, someone doesn't swear off alcohol until it's become a problem, but I'm here to tell you that's not always the case.

The reason I quit drinking wasn't because I was an alcoholic. I wasn't a drunk or out of control. I quit because I wanted to improve myself in all aspects of my life. Whether it was through health, career, or personal growth, I saw where I could be better. In giving my life a cold, hard assessment, I also saw where I could remove things that weren't serving me. One detractor stood out above all the others: alcohol.

Of course, there were plenty of excuses to keep alcohol in my life. Alcohol is the cornerstone of the modern American social life, as it certainly was for mine. My choice to quit drinking would not go unnoticed by my friends and family, and how would I justify it? Self-improvement is an ambiguous reason to give an old drinking buddy when he asks why you quit, but I had a second reason to abstain—one that anyone could understand.

My father drank himself to death. Growing up, he and I weren't particularly close, and alcohol ensured our relationship never had the chance to improve. After my father retired, he spent the rest of his life in an alcohol-induced haze, until eventually his body and mind wasted away. He wasn't the only one in my family with a weakness for alcohol. Both my grandfathers had to give up alcohol at some point in their lives, and I even had a great-grandfather who was locked away in, as it was called, an inebriate asylum. The risk of becoming an alcoholic ran thick in my blood.

Genetics are powerful, but so is free will, and I resolved to break the cycle. Now that I have kids of my own, avoiding my father's fate is more important to me than ever. I swore I'd be a better father to them than mine ever was to me, because it's a sad thing for a son to look back at his father's life and only have one thought: "What a waste." I don't think I would've ever gone down the same path as my father, but I knew it was better to remove the obstacle rather than risk tripping over it.

All of this isn't to say that I never made mistakes under the influence of alcohol. Nearly everybody who drinks regularly can look back at their past and regret an alcohol-induced decision. Personally, I looked back at my history with alcohol and realized it was the one thing I could quit that would improve most situations. So, I told myself, let's try it.

A LIFETIME OF DRINKING

For me, deciding to stop drinking was no small lifestyle change. I drank regularly, downing a couple glasses of wine or tumblers of Tito's vodka every night. I wouldn't get drunk, but I always had a drink in hand, and if you asked me how long it had been since I'd gone a day without at least a nightcap, I honestly couldn't tell you. Alcohol had been in my life since before I was old enough to buy myself a beer.

I was about fourteen years old and at my buddy Dan's house the first time I ever got a buzz from drinking. We stole his stepmom's wine coolers and snuck them out back. It didn't take much; just two of the coolers did the trick for me. We finished our drinks and then rode push scooters around the neighborhood. I remember gliding along the sidewalk, feeling great, when a tree branch hanging over the sidewalk cracked me in the head. The branch knocked me to the ground, and I wondered why I was so dizzy. I also thought, "This is kind of fun."

So, it began. After that day, my friends and I drank every now and then when we got our hands on some beer. My drinking habits only escalated from there. By the time I was a junior in high school, I could split a case with a friend. We'd drink and drive and generally be irresponsible teenagers. After high school, I graduated to the pros. I started bartending in some of Detroit's bigger nightclubs. For the next decade, alcohol was literally the foundation of my livelihood. Every night was a party where I drank and did shots, and trips with my friends were always centered around alcohol. All the time, life was drink, drink, drink, drink.

Over time, the unthinkable happened: I grew sick of the cycle of partying, drinking, and chasing women. Here I was, living a life that, to many young men, would seem like a dream, and it had lost its appeal. When I met my wife, I knew I had to give up my life of debauchery if I wanted to keep her. She helped get me on the right track, but even together, we drank a lot. If we were going to a concert, sporting event, or holiday party, we were also going out drinking.

Around the same time that I met my wife, I left the bar industry and began working in mortgages. I wasn't drinking during work anymore, but I'd still regularly go out for happy hour. Little by little, alcohol played a smaller role in my life, but it maintained an almost daily presence. A real turning point came when I discovered a passion in my late twenties that was completely incompatible with drinking: competitive bodybuilding. When every ounce of body fat matters, alcohol—even one drink—can be detrimental to your progress.

I obsessed over performing my best. I'd go to the gym every night, cook all my meals at home, and consume much less alcohol. Hard work and a strict regimen allowed me to make noticeable progress day by day. After a week of working out, I'd look awesome by Friday morning, but if I decided to go out on Friday night and have a couple drinks, I'd wake up Saturday looking just like I did on Monday. Alcohol had a way of setting back the clock.

I only had one choice if I wanted to become a national-level bodybuilder: I had to pull alcohol from my life. I'd reached a point where my hard work paid off in a major way—I was a MuscleTech-sponsored athlete and did fitness modeling ads—and I had to ask myself if a few hours of instant gratification on Friday night was worth the daily feeling of screwing up my goals. Living as a competitive athlete drove me away from alcohol for a while, but after I stopped bodybuilding and switched to working on the industry side of fitness, I started drinking again.

WHAT MADE ME QUIT FOR GOOD

No one thing in particular made me quit drinking. Rather, the decision was the sum of many smaller parts. I quit because I looked at my path to success and at the things I value most in life: my family, running my two companies, staying fit, and spending quality time with my kids. I wanted to do better, and I realized the key to success often lies in self-control.

Some people go with the flow, unconcerned when they cheat on their diet or stay up later than they promised. I am not one of those people. The second I feel I've lost my self-control over something, I'm done with it. One of those things was tobacco.

I loved tobacco and regularly chewed until one day my habit came to an abrupt end. I quit during a trip to Australia with my wife. We were out to dinner with the CFO of a Fortune 50 company, talking shop and having an engaging conversation. Later that night, I reflected on spending time with the CFO, an undeniably intelligent and successful man, and I asked myself, would I talk to him with chew in my mouth?

The answer was "Hell no." That's not who I am. The person I am, and who I want to be, is a man who doesn't feel out of place in a Fortune 50 CFO's company. However, I can't be that man with a piece of chew in my mouth, so I quit chewing that day and never chewed again. Having the self-control to give up chew was something I knew would improve my life, and alcohol was ultimately a similar issue.

After a long history of teetering on the edge of control, the only way to maintain complete authority over my drinking was to be done with it entirely. Clearheaded, I'm bulletproof. With alcohol involved, we're all susceptible to weak moments. I wasn't willing to take unnecessary risks or make myself more vulnerable to bad choices. Whether it's drinking and driving, texting an ex, or saying something stupid to a coworker, alcohol makes it easier to slip up.

It only takes one bad night of drinking to destroy your life. Between my family and career, the stakes were too high, so I chose to wipe the possibility of "one bad night" completely off the table. As an investor and entrepreneur, I already swim in risk every day. I drink uncertainty for breakfast, lunch, and dinner. If there's something like alcohol that I can remove in order to operate more competently and be more in control, you bet I'm going to purge it.

In the back of my mind, I always thought I'd like to stop drinking, but I didn't know how to quit. Mostly, I'd resisted taking the leap because of the pervasive belief that quitting means surrendering, retreating, and saying, "I failed." I struggled with the idea of admitting defeat, and I think a lot of other people do, too.

However, when people give in to the fear of retreating, they wind up waiting for things to get out of control before they stop drinking. Maybe they receive a DUI, lose their job, or end up in rehab—events that force them to quit and take away their choice in the matter—or otherwise hit rock-bottom. When I thought about giving up alcohol, I knew, objectively, I wasn't failing; I was quitting while I was ahead. Once I overcame the negative associations of giving up alcohol, I felt completely confident in my decision.

EVERYONE EXPECTS YOU TO DRINK

Once you've made the decision to give up alcohol, your next thought might be, "This is going to be hard." You wouldn't be wrong. Not drinking gets easier the longer you do it, but quitting in the first place can be difficult.

The transition period during which you need to explain to your friends—and sometimes yourself—why you're not drinking will test your resolve the most.

One Saturday morning at the gym, a friend mentioned he'd quit drinking for Lent. I asked him if cutting out alcohol was hard. His answer? "Absolutely." He pointed out one of the most challenging hurdles: not drinking can feel socially awkward. After a while, life without alcohol is normal, but until then, it's easy to feel like a social outlier. For many people, alcohol is par for the course, an assumed part of social situations. Without a drink in hand, there's a void.

I'm a big believer in questioning why we do what we do. Most of the time, it seems we do what's in front of us. For many people, myself included, that means drinking. I genuinely enjoyed alcohol and the particulars that go along with it, like appreciating craft beers or wines from different regions. What I didn't enjoy was the social obligation of drinking, the risk, and the nagging suspicion that I was only drinking because everyone else was, too.

Now that I've cut alcohol out of my life, I don't miss it. I definitely don't miss the hangovers, not that I got them often. Somehow, rarely feeling hungover was troubling in its own way. Some people have a drink or two and get dizzy, but my body didn't reject the alcohol. The drinks went down easy; I didn't want to make it easier.

Even though I've quit, I'm not antialcohol; I simply have no use for it in my life. Many people assume they need to drink and would be surprised by the fact that they don't. It's not necessary, and if you ask anybody who's had issues with alcohol, "Would you have given up drinking to avoid this consequence?" most of them will say yes. Don't get me wrong, I know and understand the appeal of drinking. There are four major things we want as humans: food, water, sex, and to get out of our minds. Alcohol helps us escape.

My go-to escape after a long workday was a glass of Tito's vodka on the rocks. Depending on my social obligations, I might have had three or four in one evening. Most nights, I would just drink enough to knock the edge off, but when I was out with other people, I often took my consumption further. We all tend to drink more in social situations. Once you pour a drink, you might feel like you can laugh a little more or say some things you wouldn't normally let slip. It opens up a social door that, in a way, gives us permission to be free and act differently than we're expected to act the rest of our day, and that includes pouring another drink.

There's a saying that epitomizes the social-alcohol phenomenon: "Anybody dancing sober is insane." Maybe it helps to have some liquid courage before dancing. We have many pithy adages that reinforce the belief that we need alcohol to allow ourselves to do or say certain things. For example, say there's a person you find attractive. You might feel that if you came right out and expressed your attraction, you'd come off as too forward. However, get a couple drinks involved between the two of you and there's an unspoken social agreement that it's now much more acceptable to express yourselves in a manner that you previously didn't feel comfortable. Similarly, you can take a group of sober guys, put them in a room, and they'll have a conversation. Put drinks in front of them, and they'll be high fiving and hugging, because alcohol can make us more comfortable with that behavior and generally bring people closer.

YOU CAN'T STAY SHARP IF YOU DULL YOURSELF DOWN

Ultimately, deciding to quit drinking was simple for me: I wanted to be on top of my game more than I wanted alcohol. When you have to take calls at midnight, run a business, and be up at six o'clock for a meeting, you can't afford to be intoxicated. I regularly see people jeopardize future opportunities in networking and business situations because of alcohol, and I never want to put myself in that scenario. My goals are to be healthy, in shape, smart, compassionate, and caring. Alcohol helps with none of those.

When you live a high-stress life, alcohol is an easy way to release some of the pressure or extend the periods when you're feeling relaxed. We drink when things are good, and we drink when things are bad. My dad basically drowned himself in alcohol because he didn't want to deal with his problems. You know what? Problems don't cease to exist because you go out drinking. They'll be there in the morning, worse than ever. You're much better off accepting that there's a problem and charging it like a bull. Personally, I don't care if it's midnight when a problem arises; I'm not going to sleep until I solve it.

Since I quit, I'm more confident in my performance and the direction of my life, because I know my thought process is clear. You can be confident, too, but you have to realize that the allure of alcohol is all in your head. You don't need it. All it does is poison your brain into feeling numb or more comfortable in certain situations. When I coach people on their diets, I tell them the same thing. It's just food. Your hunger for junk is your brain telling you that fat, salt, sugar, and alcohol make you feel good, but you don't need them. Whether you want to unwind, destress, or feel more comfortable in social situations, there are better ways to do it.

When I think about what in my life is different now, the answer is both everything and nothing. Realizing I didn't need alcohol and finding the strength to remove it from my life was empowering. Regarding my wife and children, eliminating the potential of alcohol-related situations going sideways was a way for me to make a major commitment to our life together. Compared to fifteen years ago, I live a completely different lifestyle today, and the value I place on alcohol in my daily life has dropped to zero. There are times when I think it might be nice to have a drink, but there are many more times when I couldn't care less that I'm not drinking.

I think my wife misses sharing a glass of wine over dinner, but the upside is that my family situation is stronger than it's ever been. My business is at its peak. The first thirty days after I quit drinking were the best month I've ever had with one of my companies and led to some major breakthroughs with the other. My mind had never been clearer. On top of all that, waking up ready to hit the gym and deal with whatever the day throws at me never gets old.

BE A METICULOUS MOTHER******

Nothing has helped me more with quitting drinking than fully embracing the fact that I'm a control freak. Being an intense person and putting a lot of pressure on myself is written into my DNA, and that side of my personality has served me well. As I mentioned before, my life has no shortage of stress. In the past, I used to lighten the load with alcohol, but releasing pressure from a chemical standpoint isn't healthy, nor is it a long-term solution. Worst of all, drinking to mitigate stress can damage you and the people you love. You're much better off doing things like yoga, meditation, and self-affirmation to get your stress under control. I was never open to any of those things before I quit drinking.

Another habit that has helped me quit drinking is staying organized. Life is chaos, so when you have the opportunity to keep something under control and in order, take it. Staying organized can be as simple as managing your time. For example, if I'm going somewhere with my family, I'll plan when we want to leave and arrive. We use the acronym "AIS" in my house, which stands for "Ass in Seat." If I say to my kids, "Hey, AIS, 4:10," everybody knows to be in the car at 4:10. I'm on top of the schedule to get the best results. On the flip side, if I get stuck in traffic, it won't phase me. It used to, but part of trying to be better is accepting that you can't control everything.

While it's not possible to control everything, you can control yourself. I've found there are four key factors to reaching the promised land of a better life: self-control, discipline, gratitude, and perspective. If you can master those four qualities, you can be the master of your world. The first two are the most important when it comes to quitting alcohol. Self-control is saying no when a friend pressures you to drink; discipline is waking up every morning and reaffirming your decision. Alcohol is the opposite of self-control and discipline, and with it, everything is harder.

Getting to where I am now wasn't easy—I didn't have a book to help me figure it out—and I want to make it simpler for you to achieve more in your life by living alcohol-free. Some people aren't ready to draw a line in the sand and give up alcohol entirely, but often, drawing a line is what works. If you don't draw a line, you're left with a gray area, wondering, "How many drinks is too many?" and that's a slippery slope.

If you're serious about making changes, there are two things you need to do: be relentless about your decision and cut the sh*t. We all know what the sh*t is. It's the excuses we make and the mind games we play with ourselves to justify behavior such as having a cheat meal, skipping a day at the gym, or having that beer during Monday night football when you promised yourself you were only going to drink on the weekend. Cut it and be relentless with your decision.

I expect the best from myself, and I've found that not drinking results in my best performance. I'm sure you want the best from yourself, too, so ask yourself if alcohol is holding you back. Can you achieve more professionally and personally by being alcohol-free or more alcohol aware? I'd be willing to bet the answer is yes.

CHAPTER ONE

ALCOHOL AS A SOCIAL OBLIGATION

Alcohol is everywhere. We as a society are so comfortable with it that drinking is an unspoken rite of passage, even for underage people. We grow up seeing alcohol as a social habit, and even an obligation. Whether we're tailgating, going to college parties, or attending a birthday party, alcohol is all around us and an expected part of social interaction—and I think that's a serious problem.

We've become overly comfortable with alcohol to the point where we treat it differently from other mind-altering substances. For example, marijuana has a stigma attached to it. Some people talk about pot like it's as dangerous as heroin, yet those same people will drink a couple glasses of wine every night. However, when you look at the amount of problems caused by alcohol, from drinking and driving to alcoholism, giving it special treatment doesn't make sense. I actually believe that alcohol is the real gateway drug.

What happened that caused us to put alcohol on a pedestal? We can thank, in large part, its commercialization. Whether you see alcohol on television or attend a beer-sponsored sporting event, the alcohol industry has done an excellent job of advertising its products. Humans are comfortable with the familiar, and we know alcohol on a first-name basis.

Drinking is the de facto social lubricant for nearly every social situation. We drink together to unwind, to celebrate, and to lament. In certain situations, alcohol is such an expected part of the event, it's considered odd to not have a drink. That's where we have things backwards as a society. Consider that part of the social obligation when you meet friends for dinner is that everyone orders a drink. If you don't, those drinking around you may feel uncomfortable, and you risk becoming the outsider at the table.

The social obligation of alcohol is one of the most common reasons people don't quit drinking and, for some, the only reason they drink at all. A friend of mine almost never drinks. He doesn't enjoy alcohol, and the only time he ever consumes it is when he feels socially obligated. If he's at a bar with people and someone puts a beer in his hand, he won't refuse the drink, but he also doesn't want it. He'll sip the beer and carry it around for two hours, but only because he knows that not doing so would make people—including himself—uncomfortable. Carrying around a beer you don't want seems funny, but I completely understand his reasoning.

Since I cut alcohol out of my life, I've had to turn down drinks, something that can be especially difficult in situations that induce worry or awkwardness. When this happens, it's important to be strong and hold your ground. It's okay to say, "I'm good. I don't need a drink." It's unfortunate that we're generally so comfortable with alcohol that it's actually uncomfortable to not drink, but ultimately the choice is still yours.

WHEN EVENTS ARE ACTUALLY DRINKING EVENTS

In and around Detroit, we have a huge opening day celebration for the Tigers, and for many people every year, it's an absolute sh*t show—so many people look at the event as an opportunity to start drinking early and go all day long. Anyone who's been to a sporting event knows excessive alcohol consumption isn't limited to baseball.

I took my son to an afternoon Red Wings game, and the crowd was getting rowdy. The referee made a call against the team and the whole crowd yelled, "Bullsh*t! Bullsh*t!" My son cracked up and thought it was hilarious, but it made me think about the group dynamics of alcohol. Drinking leads to people acting in ways they normally wouldn't—most people wouldn't start shouting "bullsh*t" if they were alone. The results of overindulging aren't always harmless, even at a sporting event. Sometimes, excessive drinking leads to danger beyond enjoyment. I've witnessed many fights break out, and even when venues take measures to limit consumption, such as implementing two-drinks-per-person rules, alcohol often still ends up being a problem.

Drinking dominates not only our sports, but our holidays. If you picture a New Year's Eve party, what is the most iconic image? Toasting with champagne at midnight. St. Patrick's Day, for many people, is solely a drinking holiday, defined by green beer and all-day bingeing. Consequently, people who normally wouldn't drink excessively or wouldn't drink during the day get swept up in the hype and make bad decisions.

Indeed, it seems few events are too holy for obligatory

drinking. I learned this firsthand when I went to a Christmas party with some friends of my wife's family. It was one o'clock in the afternoon, the day after Christmas, and everyone was drinking except me. In the first thirty minutes alone, I was asked five times if I wanted a drink, and not by different people. I kept saying, "No, I'm okay."

Finally, my mother-in-law told the insistent host, "Adam doesn't drink alcohol. He gave it up." Her announcement almost made the situation more awkward, but she'd felt as uncomfortable as I had, hearing drink after drink being offered to me. Why couldn't the overly gracious host accept my refusal? We've conditioned ourselves to believe that we all need a drink. When I told the host, "No. I'm fine," my choice clashed with their social norm.

If I'd attended the same party before I quit drinking, it would've been a very different experience. The party was mostly friends of my wife's family, a crowd that wasn't familiar or particularly comfortable to me. Most likely, I would've drunk on the excessive side, just to have something to do. Many people drink because it's a social crutch. For example, leaving a conversation to go grab a beer is something to do in an awkward situation. Alcohol fills a blank moment when you'd otherwise just be standing somewhere.

In contrast to this slow, anxious drinking is the excessive, celebratory bingeing that we often take part in, spending our birthdays intoxicating ourselves. I stopped celebrating my birthday with alcohol when I turned thirty-five because it didn't make sense to me anymore. Why would I go out and destroy myself to celebrate my birth? Literally poisoning yourself with alcohol is such a contradiction to the celebration of life.

In a terrible case of irony, I've known people who died on their twenty-first birthdays from drinking. A peer at my school celebrated his twenty-first birthday by going out drinking, but first, he primed his stomach with Pepto-Bismol. Then he threw back twenty-one shots. The medicine worked as he intended. It kept him from vomiting. Tragically, vomiting is exactly what his body needed, and because he couldn't purge his stomach, he died from alcohol poisoning. He was a smart kid, with years of playing soccer at Michigan State and a bright future ahead of him, but his entire life ended because of alcohol.

There's a societal disconnect with alcohol that needs addressing, a shift in attitude where people can say, "It's not cool to get wasted, and it's not cool to make drinking the focal point of an event." Going back to my earlier point about other drugs, we take people dying from heroin seriously. You never see a movie in which heroin turns out to be good for anybody. Yet, movies like the *American*

Pie and the *National Lampoon* series glorify young people drinking, while mostly ignoring the damage it does.

Concerts are yet another area dominated by alcohol, and I noticed something interesting about my own behavior at concerts. When I went to see my favorite bands, like the Counting Crows, Jack Johnson, and John Mayer, I didn't care to drink as much as I normally would. The reason I drank less was because I didn't want to spend half the show waiting in line for the bathroom, standing in the beer line, or too buzzed to remember the show.

On the other hand, my wife loves eighties hair bands like Tesla, Poison, and Mötley Crüe—which I don't particularly enjoy. When I used to go to those concerts, I'd drink a lot more to offset the painful experience of subjecting myself to the terrible music because, like an awkward Christmas party, I had nothing else to do but think about not wanting to be there. Alcohol made the lack of enjoyment less uncomfortable. Now that using alcohol to fill the void is no longer an option, I've found a new appreciation for concerts. Even if I don't like the music, I can appreciate that it makes other people happy, which lets me enjoy the present more and makes for great people-watching.

You expect to find alcohol at concerts and sporting events, but I've even been to a diaper party where drinking was the focal point. An old drinking buddy of mine was having a baby and invited a bunch of the guys to his house. I hadn't seen this group in a while, so it was important to me to spend time with them and catch up. I arrived at his house and found the group hanging out in the garage with the space heater on, watching the Michigan football game and playing beer pong. Mind you, everyone there was almost forty years old, if not older. I couldn't help but think, "Haven't we f**king moved on from beer pong and garage parties?"

The party would've been uncomfortable regardless, but it was even stranger going there and not drinking. I think my buddies recognized that life was working out for me, so most of them didn't give me a hard time about not drinking, except for one guy who just couldn't get over it. We had a funny—but awkward—exchange:

Buddy: You don't drink?

Me: No.

Buddy: What do you do?

Me: What do you mean?

Buddy: How do you not drink?

Me: I just don't. Don't you go days without drinking?

Buddy: Yeah.

Me: That's what I do every day.

Even though drinking is largely what brought these friends and me together in the first place, I realized we didn't need alcohol to enjoy each other's company. Aside from me not loving hanging out in a garage drinking beer anymore, our dynamic hadn't changed at its core. If drinking is the backbone of your friendships, giving up alcohol will likely be a tough hurdle to overcome, but I believe most relationships can survive the leap.

After I quit, a neighbor and good friend of mine, Joe, sent me a text that said, "Hey, you still not drinking? I wanted to see if you were up for grabbing a beer." I told him I could get a Diet Coke, but my suggestion caught him off guard. We're so conditioned to "grab a beer" that, even though Joe and I are good buddies, it seemed strange to say, "Hey, let's hang out and talk."

So much camaraderie exists around drinking that you might not notice it until the alcohol is gone. When you go out for a beer and talk about the beer list, it fills the gaps in the conversation. However, when you drink a Diet

Coke, it doesn't exactly warrant a discussion. You lose that point of connection, but bonding that happens over beer isn't necessarily about the alcohol; it's about sharing an experience. If you don't drink, it can feel like you're not in the fraternity, and I think that's why a lot of people drink when they'd rather not. The thing is, the disconnect is all in our heads. Drinking isn't needed to feel that bond, but it takes honesty and understanding from the drinkers and nondrinkers to make it work.

THE MORE YOU DRINK, THE MORE YOU DRINK

It's a simple equation: when you go out regularly, the drinking adds up. With maturity, most people can keep things in check, but the bottom line is that the more often you drink, the more drinks you're going to consume. When you drink more, you're also more likely to get into what I call the "problem zone" and make mistakes. It can be easy to fall into this trap because, so often, you might think you're going out socializing when you're actually going out drinking.

How often you drink hinges a lot on your group of friends, and you'll likely find that when you spend time with old friends, habits carry over. Suppose you're catching up with friends from college—friends you used to drink with excessively. When you were in college in your twenties, you most likely weren't accountable for as many things as you are in your thirties or forties, but it's easy to lapse back into the same old behaviors. So, you clink glasses, do shots, and drink like a college student.

Falling into old habits isn't usually too big a deal if you only see old friends occasionally, but if you start working in the same place, for example, it can be dangerous. Your comfort level from the social setting can carry over into the workplace and get you in a lot of trouble. Similarly, maybe you're at your best friend's wedding and you drink too much with your old buddies. You act like a moron, and now you're forever branded as "the guy who drinks too much" by your best friend's family.

A negative brand can hurt your self-esteem, how you identify yourself, and your comfort level around that group of friends, likely forever. The more you drink to excess, the more it beats down on your self-esteem, dragging you down a slippery slope. If drinking is part of your identity and is damaging your reputation, those are good signs that cutting out alcohol is the right move.

THE THREE TYPES OF DRINKERS

Not all drinkers are alike. Generally, people fall into one of three categories when it comes to their relationship with alcohol. The first group are people for whom alcohol is always a slippery slope. They're the people who go out to drink above any other objective for the night. Over the years, I've had many friends, especially during my time bartending, who were routinely sh*t shows whenever we went out drinking. I'm talking blackout drunk, not remembering anything, leaving their ID at the bar—when they went out to drink, it was all or nothing.

A good friend of mine fits into this category. When he came to town, I had to brace myself. He would pull up to my house with a fifth of Tito's and a twelve-pack of Labatt Blue. Every time, Labatt Blue. I hated that beer.

One day, we were drinking and I asked him, "Why do you always bring Labatt Blue?"

He said, "Isn't that your favorite beer?"

I told him, "No, it's my least favorite."

So, he asked me, "Why is it always in your fridge?"

I told him it was there because they were the same bottles of Labatt Blue he'd brought the last time he was at my house. So, we had a good laugh about it. Still to this day, he'll bring that beer just to be funny.

In addition to the Labatt Blue, he and I would throw down three or four vodkas and then go out and drink some more. I almost never drank like that on my own, but it was how he liked to get after it, so whenever he came to town, I would subconsciously decide that I was going to tear it up with him that night.

The second group includes the majority of alcohol consumers: people who drink alcohol to loosen up. They're the ones who seem to imply, "You're drinking? I'm drinking. I'm okay with saying certain out-of-character things or laughing a little bit louder." My wife fits into this category. She never gets drunk, but you can tell she's been drinking. For this midrange group, alcohol is primarily a social lubricant. The green light that tells them to let their guard down and relax.

If you fall into this second category, you should be aware of your limits. Hanging out and drinking with your friends is different from drinking with coworkers, and some jokes that you might tell in one setting might not be acceptable in the other. Most people in this category are safe, but a handful of them will slip into the first category of drinkers and develop a problem.

For the third group of people, alcohol is unnecessary in their lives. It includes people like my business partner

Matt, who just doesn't care to drink. This group is pretty far from needing to be concerned about drinking and most likely won't be reading this book.

The three types of drinkers are something to keep in mind when you're spending time in a social situation. If you find yourself surrounded by category-one drinkers, you'll be more likely to drink heavily. Consider your environment as well. There are certain places where you might expect to overindulge: Las Vegas, for example. The demeanor and dynamic of the group you're with and the atmosphere can have a huge impact on how wild your night becomes. I'm not saying you should avoid these people or places, but be extra vigilant of your alcohol consumption.

Regardless of which group of people I'm spending time with, I can engage with them better now that I don't drink. I don't have to worry about distracting things like who's going to drive or where I'm going to sleep. I'm also aware of the false sense of closeness alcohol can create and I can try to replicate that level of comfort without drinking. For people who are considering giving up alcohol but are afraid of losing the social connection, my advice is this: try it.

Just go meet up with someone, don't have anything to drink, grab a water, and talk. When I put myself into this kind of situation, I find I try to create a comfort area for the other person sooner. I make it about them, because when people drink, they usually talk more, so if no one is drinking you may have to work a little harder to get a conversation going.

LAWS AND LIQUOR

The fact that we have to be controlled by the people serving us alcohol should be a big red flag. Fundamentally, we have a problem with alcohol in society. If we have a mandatory two-drink limit at a sporting event or a concert, there is an obvious problem. If we need to card everybody, even people twice the legal drinking age, we have a problem.

My wife, who is forty years old, goes to the grocery store with our twenty-one-year-old nanny, who doesn't even drink. Every time they go to the store, my wife needs to make sure they both bring their IDs because if my wife wants to pick up a bottle of wine, they'll both be carded. It blows my mind that so many people buy alcohol for minors that we need to enforce these blanket policies. The rules are frustrating and a hassle, but at the same time I understand why they exist, and I think they're a symptom of our unhealthy relationship with drinking.

The point is that there are so many restrictions around

alcohol because a large amount of people have displayed a lack of self-control when it comes to drinking to the point where we need the state to impose control on them. We won't go so far as getting rid of alcohol because it's a huge, prosperous industry, but we have to make rules because we can't trust people to behave responsibly.

Alcohol is everywhere—it's almost hard to avoid. We have alcohol at our celebrations, on our rough days, at family gatherings, and even at church. I'm not saying this to suggest that you should give up Communion, only to illustrate the point that alcohol is all around us, and I think everyone can benefit from being more aware of its presence and of their consumption. You can start by asking yourself: Do I always have a drink in hand when I'm out with friends? It's a good question to get a pulse check on your drinking habits. If the answer is yes, think about removing alcohol in some situations. You might be surprised to find how little you actually need a drink and how much more you can enjoy social situations without one.

CHAPTER TWO

ALCOHOL AS A CRUTCH

Take the edge off.

Liquid courage.

Grab a beer and unwind.

We've all heard alcohol described as an antidote for stress. Some people drink sparingly, but when a person drinks regularly to deal with anxiety, it becomes something they need, a crutch. They weaken their coping abilities until they need alcohol as a supplement just to function. So, why do we use alcohol as a crutch? It seems like an appealing choice—and is challenging to resist—for two reasons: the external pressures and internal pressures encouraging you to drink.

Externally, you experience the social obligation of drinking when alcohol is all around you and everyone in your presence is partaking. If you don't drink, people notice. Internally, you experience the pressures of social anxiety and stress, which alcohol can quickly help mitigate. Combined, these two forces can make giving up alcohol in social situations feel like a huge challenge.

As a society, we've done a spectacular job of embedding situations that are naturally stressful with alcohol. Whether you're attending a wedding or going to a work function, being in large groups can be uncomfortable, but there's almost always alcohol there to "help." Like putting on a seat belt when you get in a car, we don't think twice about drinking at large social gatherings, and it's rare to attend an event like a wedding that doesn't have a bar.

As American Addiction Centers says, "Alcohol consumption continues to maintain a foothold so strong in American culture that it is nearly impossible to imagine life without it." In my experience, this statement couldn't be more true.

So much of what we do is built around drinking that most people aren't truly aware of how we treat intoxicating ourselves as a run-of-the-mill act. Its mainstream presence means that we're introduced to alcohol as a coping mechanism at a young age—growing up, you see Mom and Dad having a drink after work or a glass of wine at dinner to unwind. It's treated as no big deal.

Young adults don't fully understand the potential short- and long-term consequences of drinking—they see alcohol everywhere, even at the dinner table, so how dangerous could it be?—which can lead to reckless consumption. As a result, the normalcy with which we treat alcohol creates an environment where, by the time someone is twenty-one years old, or often earlier, drinking seems like the normal, expected thing to do.

WE OFTEN DRINK THE MOST WHEN WE SHOULD DRINK THE LEAST
Weddings

There are few occasions as special as a wedding. Everyone puts on their best clothes, there are flowers on the tables, and you eat the most expensive cake of your life. Outside of Vegas drive-through chapels, weddings are usually meant to be classy affairs, yet people often drink excessively to the point of embarrassing themselves. It doesn't always happen, and hopefully it's never happened to you, but we've all seen it: that one person who makes it obvious they've had too much to drink. Nothing takes a classy event down a few notches faster than a bunch of drunk people turning your celebration into club night.

Personally, a wedding is the last place I want to drink excessively, but I used to do it anyway. In general, I don't like weddings. I enjoy the ceremony, the love, the families coming together—all of those aspects are fantastic—but I don't like being forced to dance to cheesy music and sit at a table with people I barely know. I've never been a sports-and-weather guy. When someone sits next to me and starts off with, "Hey, man, you going to see the game?" I'll most likely shoot them a look that says, "Wrong guy." Frankly, I just don't give a sh*t about that kind of small talk.

I know I'm not alone in this. Tons of people hate small talk, but when you're at a wedding with a group of people you don't know, "So, how'd you meet Joe?" often feels like the only topic of conversation. When you're stuck in an uncomfortable situation having empty conversations, what do you do? For many people, the answer is "Drink."

Friends of mine who don't drink anymore have told me the number-one situation where they wish they still drank is at weddings where they don't know anyone. Weddings are rife with uncomfortable moments, and we've made alcohol our socially acceptable crutch. Finding an alternative crutch is what I've found helps the most when you're trying not to drink but want an escape.

What makes a good alternative crutch? Anything that distracts you from the social discomfort. You could aim to remember the name of every person you meet that night or try to make every person you talk to laugh. The important part is that you recognize that alcohol is a crutch, that you reject it, and that you find something else to lean on.

Work Functions

A work function is another type of situation that's uncomfortable for many people, often for the same reasons weddings can be unpleasant. You're surrounded by people, many of whom you may not know well or wouldn't choose to spend time with outside of work. Not only do you have to make small talk, but you need to worry about making a good impression on your colleagues and higher ups. Sometimes you need to put on a show. Your job may depend on it.

All of those factors add up to a lot of pressure, and some people end up being their own worst enemies by drinking too much and ruining their reputation. It's a vicious cycle in which you worry about making an idiot of yourself, so you drink to relieve the stress, which only makes you more likely to do the one thing you fear. If you fall into this trap, you can easily put your career and life as you know it in jeopardy.

I think young people are especially susceptible to this misstep. When you're fresh out of college, you may not have a good feel for the professional environment yet or even a firm understanding of your own alcohol tolerance. Additionally, more companies are adopting a laid-back, casual office culture, which might give the illusion that it's more acceptable to let loose. Here's the thing: it's not. Saying the wrong thing or doing something stupid is just as likely to get you fired or sued at a "cool" company as it is at a suit-and-tie corporation. It's important to never forget that a work function is not a social function.

AN ARTIFICIAL BOND

One of the reasons alcohol makes such an effective social crutch is that it can act as an artificial bond between two people. Using a wedding as an example again, imagine sitting at a table with a group of people you don't know. You're making chit-chat about sports, weather, and the wedding, when you decide to run to the bar. You offer to grab people drinks, and suddenly you have this connection because you're doing something nice for them. Maybe you all do a toast to the bride and groom, which gives you a shared activity that goes beyond small talk. A bond begins to form.

Those types of shared activities create the alcohol bond. It's the cheers at happy hour or complaining about work over beers. Also, when you buy someone a drink, it's an easy act of goodwill and respect. People start these connections off with good intentions.

In a sense, it's neat that something can bring people together in the way a round of drinks can, but it's unfortunate that alcohol is the glue. Often the connection can get off to a good start—you have a drink or two and cheers—but a couple hours later, when you're six beers in, the situation can start to go downhill. The quality of conversation likely declines, either on the listening side, speaking side, or both, and the next time you see that person, whatever bond you felt while you were buzzed may not exist.

Part of the reason it may feel easier to bond with someone over alcohol is that, when we're drunk, we talk about things we normally wouldn't discuss. Alcohol opens the door for a broader conversation. Sometimes, those conversations are great. Maybe you have drinks with friends and you get something off your chest, or you tell someone something positive that you may not have said otherwise.

Positive results can come from alcohol-induced conversation, but the fact that people struggle, for a multitude of reasons, to share their feelings without a crutch is a problem.

My stance is that you can get the same positive results, or even better results, if you have a conversation without drinking, but that can be extremely difficult for someone who drinks often. If you have trouble expressing yourself without alcohol, make an effort to be aware of when, what, and how you share. Is it only when you're intoxicated? If so, it might be one of the subtle red flags that alcohol is a problem for you. Subtle in the sense that you're not getting a DUI or losing your job, but relying on alcohol to open up to people affects your life.

If this describes you, your next step should be to say to yourself, "I need to try to express my feelings when I haven't been drinking." Just try it—you'll likely find that you didn't need the alcohol. However, when alcohol makes something feel easier, you can fall down the slippery slope of defaulting to the easier path every time until you're drinking every day. Don't let yourself take the easier route.

The idea of the alcohol bond is heavily reinforced by commercialization. Anyone who's ever watched the Super Bowl can confirm that the awards for the funniest, coolest, catchiest commercials often go to the alcohol brands. Some of their commercials have reached iconic status: the Budweiser frogs, Dos Equis's "Most Interesting Man in the World," Coronas on a beach. These images and ideas ingrain themselves in our minds so much so that we think, "If I go to a country music concert, I need to drink." The commercial lays out a baseline that says, "This is how we do it."

Not only are alcohol commercials memorable, but they often coin scenarios that show people bonding. For example, Bud Light's "I love you, man," commercials reinforce the idea of men bonding over beers. It's socially acceptable to say, "Let's grab a drink," whereas it can feel uncomfortable to say, "Let's get together and talk." It doesn't matter if talking is ultimately the goal of both propositions. One feels easier to suggest than the other. Now that I don't drink, I try to always create an atmosphere where people feel like they can get things off their chest; I make it clear I'm there to listen.

THE CONSEQUENCES OF USING ALCOHOL AS A CRUTCH
Money

When you drink regularly as a way to cope with uncomfortable feelings, it's only a matter of time before you have to deal with at least a few consequences. Some consequences are small; for example, alcohol is an added expense. The cost may not be much per day, but it adds up. When you buy a fifteen-dollar beer at a baseball game, another at a concert, and a fancy cocktail on date night, it adds up fast. When you drink regularly at home, it adds up even faster.

When a friend of mine stopped drinking for a month—the same friend I shared my first wine cooler with in middle school—he realized he'd saved more than one thousand dollars that month simply by not purchasing alcohol. I realized something similar when I quit. Between my wife and me, we usually drank a bottle of wine every other night, which added up to a weekly expense of as much as $150. Drinking regularly can chip away at your disposable income and savings, but other consequences are even more destructive.

Health and Lifestyle

Perhaps the most serious consequences of drinking are the repercussions on your health. Not everyone who drinks will get into a car accident or cheat on their spouse, but everyone who drinks regularly will eventually experience an alcohol-related health issue. I want to stress that health problems are not reserved for the excessive drinker; even a small amount of alcohol can impact your health.

The most chilling effects of alcohol, in my opinion, are those on your mind. According to researchers at Rutgers University, "Performance by social drinkers on tests of abstracting and adaptive abilities was negatively associated with the amount of alcohol consumed per drinking occasion. The pattern was strongest in heavy drinkers but was also evident in light and moderate drinkers." I've witnessed this effect firsthand with my father. As I mentioned before, drinking eventually killed him, but in the last years of his life, the biggest consequence he experienced was alcohol-onset dementia. The issue manifested in such a way that, even when he was sober, he acted like he was drunk. Alcohol had permanently damaged his mental capacity.

My father drank heavily, but chronic drinkers, by which I mean the person who has two or three drinks every day, can experience severe effects as well. If you drink regularly, ask yourself, how often do you walk into a room and forget why? How often can you not find your keys? How often do you look at the time on your phone and need to check again immediately after?

We don't always realize these little mental gaffes might be related to drinking. They happen to everybody, but if you're only in your midthirties and find yourself frequently losing track of things, you may want to take a closer look.

If alcohol is the cause and you continue drinking, what state is your mind going to be in when you're seventy?

Alcohol, of course, affects nearly every organ system in your body. Here are a few examples of health consequences, some of which might surprise you:

- Mild to moderate dehydration results in deteriorated cognitive functions and desiccated skin.
- Occasional to moderate drinkers experience memory impairment, blackouts, recklessness, and impaired decision-making.
- Heavy and chronic drinkers experience diminished brain size, loss of abstract-thinking capability, decreased visuospatial abilities, memory loss, anxiety, nerve disorders, thiamine deficiency, and impaired attention span.
- Elevated estrogen levels and zinc deficiency due to alcohol consumption result in hair loss.
- A drink a day averages approximately 200 empty calories. If you didn't burn off those extra calories, you would gain roughly two pounds a month.
- Alcohol inhibits protein synthesis and starves the muscles of water.

The statistics around alcohol consumption are nearly as shocking as the health effects. The 2013 National Survey on Drug Use and Health came to the following conclusions about Americans ages twelve and older:

- Approximately 52.2 percent of the population (136.8 million people) are current alcohol users.
- Nearly 6.3 percent of the population (16.5 million people) are heavy alcohol users.
- In the past thirty days, 22.9 percent of the population (60.1 million people) reported binge-drinking behavior.
- Approximately 10.9 percent of the population (28.6 million people) reported having driven a car under the influence at least once in the past year.

When nearly a quarter of the country is binge drinking, it's safe to say we have a serious problem. We just don't view it as a problem. How much binge drinking behavior happens while watching a football game? On St. Patrick's Day? During Cinco de Mayo? We don't think twice about the person who gets hammered and just eats tacos.

Binge drinking slips under the radar, but everyone can unanimously agree that drunk driving is bad. When one in ten people is driving under the influence, that's a lot of dangerous drivers on the road, and there's going to be some overlap with the binge drinkers. All of these issues are connected, and we need to make sure we don't view the worst outcomes as though they aren't related to the widespread culture of "harmless" drinking.

Career

Earlier I discussed why people use alcohol as a crutch during work functions, but now I'd like to take a closer look at the consequences. A work environment is one of the few places where everyone is an adult and where a party atmosphere has no place. Leave the party lifestyle back in college, or at least keep it out of the office, because when you start your career, you enter the build phase of your life.

Drinking stops people from exploring greater opportunities. I'm not necessarily talking about drinking at work functions—although that can certainly bar you from opportunities as well—but being a weekend warrior or drinking after work every day can hold you back from pursuing additional goals in life. Consider that if you're the type of person who parties hard on the weekend, you'll be distracted on Friday and not particularly sharp on Monday. By Tuesday, you've probably recovered; by Wednesday, you're top-notch; by Thursday, you might be going out that night or already thinking about the weekend.

When Friday rolls around, you're more focused on thinking about the weekend than finishing your tasks for the week. Then you lose the weekend as a time for anything productive, and on Monday, you're hungover. This is a common cycle, especially for young people who may be holding on to the college lifestyle, and it kills productivity.

Drinking in any capacity at work has the potential to damage your reputation. For example, a friend of mine relayed the story of a company vacation function he attended. The group, which included high-ranking executives, was on a bus returning from an excursion when one of the salespeople who'd had too much to drink said some obnoxious things. She didn't say anything nasty or antagonizing, but she wasn't acting with any degree of professionalism or awareness of her peers.

That night sealed the salesperson's fate. She had aspired to become a manager and had been on track to do so, but her actions ensured that she would never move up in the company. She couldn't be trusted. If she hadn't drunk that night, she may have stayed at the company for years, but with one move, she'd severely damaged her chances to progress her career and guaranteed that she'd need to switch companies to advance.

Another friend of mine has a wildly successful business, but he also likes to party. To help mitigate his risk, he actually has someone on his staff whose job it is to remove him from parties if he gets too drunk and to make sure he doesn't cross any lines—a party babysitter. They get him to bed, make sure he stays, give him bottles of Fiji and aspirin, and get his ass up in the morning when he needs to get to work. It's a full babysitting service, all because he doesn't trust himself with alcohol. He knows that if he's left unsupervised, he'll drink until six in the morning and hook up with one of the salespeople, or something equally damaging. He lives in Silicon Valley and has the money to hire somebody, but most people don't.

If you rely on yourself to keep you from doing something career-threatening while drinking, I have news for you: drunk you is not reliable. If you drink too much at work functions, it will catch up to you.

I've seen drinking cause smart people to make terrible decisions. I had to fire two executives from one of my companies because they drank and hooked up with each other continually. When it became a problem, I should have fired them on the spot, but I gave them a chance. I figured that maybe the two of them would be extra motivated about work and spend their time together talking about the company.

The opposite happened. They didn't seem to think about

work at all, and their productivity took a huge hit, so I had to let them go. Often, situations like theirs—in which two people who shouldn't hook up get together—start with alcohol and spiral out of control from there. At least in their situation, all they lost were their jobs, but if a leader in an organization hooks up with a direct report, they open themselves up to massive legal problems. Almost every single time it happens, alcohol is involved.

I've witnessed people acting in the worst way possible at work, but I've also seen people who are role models. One of the people who inspired me to stop drinking is Dan Mullally. He's the senior vice president of a Fortune 50 company, and he's both smart and charismatic, the kind of guy who remembers the name of everybody in the room. When I asked him why he quit drinking, he said, "I need to be sharp 24/7, and function at 100 percent, 100 percent of the time." His reason made absolute sense to me.

One of my best friends, Marty, was in the same situation as Dan. He set high goals for himself and realized alcohol didn't fit into his plan, so he cut it from his life. I've noticed that Dan, Marty, and I have a commonality, which is this: we're all-or-nothing. Whether it's quitting alcohol, building a business, or hanging out with family, I'm going to be completely immersed and give it 100 percent.

I think the all-or-nothing personality type is the reason some people have a borderline, gray-area drinking problem. It's likely the same reason you see a lot of successful people struggle with alcohol; the same drive that allows them to build a business compels them to drink too much. They don't necessarily have anxiety issues or depression that they're medicating with alcohol, but if they're going out drinking, they're going out *drinking*. They're not going to have a few glasses of Chardonnay and call it a night. People with this personality type need to recognize this in themselves and be aware of their potential for alcohol abuse.

Personally, I had a hard time navigating the work/party balance earlier in my career. My first office job was at Quicken Loans, and I worked on a relatively young team. Everybody was wired to go hard. We'd work twelve-hour days, grinding our faces off, but when we left work, guess what happened? We grinded our faces off at the bar, too. Working hard and partying hard created an ugly cycle. You can only maintain that lifestyle for so long until it wears you down.

When I was little older and my wife and I would attend work functions together, we had a two-drinks-per-hour rule. We'd watch out for each other, and if one of us started acting goofy, the other would give the signal that it was time to go. Having someone trustworthy monitor your alcohol intake is a stopgap solution to workplace slipups, but the only way to make sure you're airtight is to not drink.

Relationships

The role alcohol plays in relationships can be good, or at least neutral, as I discussed earlier. If all of your activities with a particular friend revolve around drinking, the reliance on alcohol may keep your relationship from deepening, but it's mostly harmless. The fact remains that we can have those same friendships and conversations without drinking. The amazing thing about removing alcohol is that everything is real; you're not filtering your thoughts and words through alcohol.

The alcohol filter might make someone laugh harder at your jokes, but it also amplifies the negative aspects of a relationship. Alcohol fuels miscommunication. Anything someone finds offensive or misinterprets will come off even worse after a few drinks. For example, an argument between a couple has never improved because they added alcohol to the equation.

One of my best friends, who I used to drink with, gave up alcohol as well. We were two intense personalities, and we used to go out and tear it up. We'd also go out with our wives to dinner or a concert and share a couple bottles of wine. This was in the age before Uber, so we had a neighbor we'd pay one hundred dollars to drive us around because we knew we wouldn't be fit to drive by the end of the night.

Unfortunately, when we went out with my friend and his wife, they would often get into fights. They'd drink, get upset, and say hurtful things to each other. The next day, they wouldn't be angry when they woke up, and sometimes they couldn't even recall what their argument had been about. However, their fighting created an awkward environment for my wife and me, so we'd try to scale back the drinking in the hopes that they would avoid a confrontation.

Over time, that added layer of anxiety made us hesitant to go out with them at all. We cared about them because they were our friends, but it was hard seeing them have ugly, alcohol-fueled fights. Alcohol, in general, weakened all our relationships, and it had never been more apparent how drinking can bring sloppy, hurtful emotions to the surface.

I caught up with that friend after I quit drinking, and we laughed about our wild times together, but we also had some deep, intellectual conversations. Talking with him was better than ever, I think, because we both realized we didn't need alcohol to take that deep dive. We'd both been down the same path of removing alcohol, and in going down that path, we'd dealt with a lot of self-truths. Nobody decides to quit drinking without some quality introspection. Dealing with your self-truths in turn allows you to bring more truth and authenticity to your relationships.

In the same way that alcohol can hold your career back, it can also hinder your relationships. In general, people shouldn't drink when they're at their saddest, their happiest, or feeling any extreme emotion—especially if that emotion is anger—but ironically, that's when we usually drink the most. Alcohol amplifies all emotions and emboldens people to do things they normally wouldn't even consider, which is often a bad thing. There's a reason they wouldn't normally do those things.

For example, back when I worked in the mortgage industry, I had a coworker who I would grab drinks with every now and then. He was as normal as anyone could be, the kind of person who wouldn't stand out in a crowd. That was, until he drank.

When he drank, he became one of the weirdest, most awkward people I've ever met. More than anything, he became loud and physical. Happy hour would turn into a sitcom situation. Our group would be hanging out, drinking, and shooting the sh*t, and then this guy would start acting off-the-wall. The alcohol just didn't agree with him.

After it became obvious that drinking around this guy was a bad time, my coworkers and I would invite him to lunch, but never to drinks. Occasionally, he'd show up to happy hour anyway and awkwardly say, "Hey, I didn't know you guys were coming here." The rest of us would be thinking, "Oh sh*t, what's he going to do?" He probably would've been accepted into the group with no problem if he didn't drink, or at least didn't drink as much.

Alcohol does strange things to people, and unfortunately, they usually don't even know it. Nobody but your most brutally honest friend is going to tell you that you're drinking too much, or that you get weird after a few drinks. It's like having bad breath—you could fix it if you knew there was a problem. Fixing the problem might dramatically change your life for the better, but nobody tells you because they don't want to risk hurting your feelings. People don't want the confrontation, so instead, they might avoid you.

Telling hard truths is almost as difficult as hearing them. Even when you'd be doing someone a justice by being honest with them, there isn't a good way to do this unless they're a close friend. I could have said to my coworker, "Hey, bro, you need to chill with the drinking," but that would have been extremely awkward.

When this guy would get a few drinks in him and start putting his hands on people's shoulders, I couldn't help but wonder why he felt so overly comfortable. Later, I realized that alcohol changes social dynamics between people. For example, if you're someone's superior in some sense and put your arm around them when you drink, it changes the dynamic. Even if it's nothing but a buddy arm, it's an action that wouldn't have happened without alcohol and wouldn't have left anyone feeling uncomfortable.

If you're slightly intoxicated—feeling happy, warm, good— and you throw your arm around someone who doesn't like it, there are no positive outcomes. In the best-case scenario, your relationship will be weird going forward. In the worst-case scenario, the other person will take serious offense and file a complaint. The point is that even tiny actions that seem harmless can quickly make a relationship uncomfortable; removing alcohol from the situation lessens the chance of that happening.

The type of awkward social environment I'm describing can happen anywhere. I've seen men go out to a restaurant and be completely respectful to the attractive female wait staff, but after a few drinks, they start calling the server "honey" and trying to hold her hand. Women do it too—when I used to work in nightclubs, there were many instances when women tried to buy me a drink and wound up acting inappropriately beyond belief before they'd left for the evening.

Alcohol makes you feel good, and it tricks you into thinking everyone else feels good, too. That's a fallacy, because, most likely, the other person isn't on the same page. I can't think of a better example than one year at Christmastime when my wife and I went to a neighbor's party. There were about a dozen people there. Half were our neighbors; the other half were the host's coworkers. We played White Elephant, and because the party was adults-only, some people brought funny gifts.

Everybody at the party had downed a few drinks and was having a good time, but there was one man there who I'd never met before. Right off the bat, he gave me a weird vibe, like he had a chip on his shoulder. At some point, he looked at my shoes and asked, "Those Ferragamo or Cole Haan?"

I told him "Cole Haan," and he just replied, "Figures."

This was a strange thing to say, but I didn't think much of it. I could tell he was on his way to being intoxicated.

Like I said, it was a small party, so I couldn't exactly dodge this guy. He was probably in his midforties, and when I overheard that he was in the middle of a divorce—all the more reason he shouldn't have been drinking—his state made more sense. However, it didn't make him any less awkward. By the time we were halfway through the White Elephant gifts, this guy was drunk. At that point, the raciest gift anyone had opened was his-and-her lube. Then we get to this guy's gift.

It was an obvious and inappropriate sex toy for the present company. We went from relatively tame gifts to a giant sex toy. Suffice it to say that everyone at the party was shocked. He was clearly the only person who didn't realize how inappropriate his gift and actions were. The situation got worse when the guy wanted to keep the gift that he'd brought! He walked around the party making inappropriate gestures to other people's wives. All the while, I was watching this happen and thinking, "What the hell is wrong with this guy?"

He tried to leave while still drunk, and my neighbor had to take his keys. No one wanted him to stay at the house, but we couldn't let him drive drunk and run somebody over, either. The whole situation was a mess.

The next day, I asked my neighbor what was up with that guy, and he was at a loss.

He said, "Usually, he's the most normal person I've ever met—but I've never gone out drinking with him before."

With just a few drinks, the guy had made an absolute fool of himself and made an entire houseful of people uncomfortable. I look back on that night and think two things: (1) you never want to be that guy, and (2) you never want that guy around. Sometimes, there's nothing in a person's brain that tells them, "This is a bad idea. I'm making everybody uncomfortable," and I think alcohol is often to blame.

Individuality

You can take a table full of strangers, put a bottle of booze in between them, and suddenly, they'll all be singing a song together. Sounds great, right? Not necessarily. With a similar mechanism to false bonds, alcohol creates a herd environment. People get together and drink with alcohol being the obvious commonality; these people stop being individuals and become a group.

Imagine you're out drinking with friends. You're ready to call it a night when someone says, "Let's stop at Smith's up the street and grab one more drink."

You could follow your own inclinations and leave early,

but it's a lot easier socially to go along for the last drink. In that way, alcohol can bring a group closer together, but it can also make you fall into a place where you wouldn't have gone without the alcohol. The effect is akin to peer pressure, only subtler and less nefarious.

Maybe your friend asks if you want to grab a drink, and you know you're going to have to drive them home because they'll drink three martinis in an hour. You don't want to say yes, but you'd feel guilty saying no. Or, maybe your friend calls you and says they just broke up with their partner. You go out to talk with them and have a quick glass of wine, but the next thing you know, you've split three bottles, it's one in the morning, and you have work the next day.

You can get sucked in to unpleasant situations, and sometimes downright dangerous ones. Riots, bar brawls, and group fights at sporting events are usually fueled by alcohol, because when you're intoxicated, it's easy to stop thinking like an individual. You can't be your best if you're not an individual first.

Alcohol is America's favorite social crutch, so the biggest challenge is to not engage. Don't count your drinks or restrict yourself to one drink every two hours. Just don't drink. The first step to improving yourself is taking on the challenge and seeing if you can do it, so give it a try. Whether you're successful or not, trying to cut out drinking altogether allows you to get a grasp on where you are in terms of relying on alcohol.

In the same way that we take tests in school or do blood work during physicals, you need to touch base with yourself. One of the reasons I quit drinking was because I looked at my past, at myself, and at the direction I was heading, and what I saw disturbed me.

The key is to recognize that you don't have to feel obligated to drink alcohol, no matter what the situation and no matter how many other people are drinking. A lot of people say they don't need to drink to have fun—if you believe that about yourself, put your money where your mouth is and see if you're up to the challenge.

CHAPTER THREE

WHY I QUIT

When you decide to quit drinking, you need to have a strong "why." Your "why" is what's going to keep you motivated when something or someone challenges your resolve, or when the challenge loses its excitement. The "why" is the difference between people seeing their goals through and giving up on them.

Your reason for quitting doesn't have to be dramatic or complicated; it can be a desire for self-improvement, as it was for me. I'm constantly performing A/B testing in my life to see what I can improve because I want to be a better husband, a better dad, and so on. As a society, I don't think we take as much time for self-assessment as we should, and alcohol moves us further away from that goal.

If you want to hustle and grow your life, first and foremost, you need to examine how you spend your time. A prominent marketing guru, Gary Vaynerchuk, wisely advises that you audit your seven to ten. This means you need to think about what you're doing every day between 7:00 p.m. and 10:00 p.m. Are you spending your evenings moving closer to your goals, or are you spending them watching television?

I don't generally have much free time; I do a lot with my family, work out five to six days a week, and attend a lot of social events. Making time for other activities is, as it is for so many people, a constant challenge. Typically, before I quit drinking, I'd spend time with my family from around 7:00 p.m. to 8:30 p.m. and then I'd work. However, while I worked, I'd drink. My nutrition, sleep, physical fitness, work habits, and general well-being were all good, but when I audited my seven to ten, I realized alcohol potentially held me back from moving toward my goals as much as I could. To my productivity, alcohol was public enemy number one.

The same parts of my personality—my drive and focus—that allowed me to excel in bodybuilding and business were the same qualities that pushed me to drink too much. If I went out drinking, I drank hard. My strong personality backfired, so to speak, which is why I decided I had to quit drinking, full stop.

When I first cut out alcohol, my father-in-law asked me, "Why can't you just drink in moderation?"

I told him, "Ray, I don't do anything in moderation. I'm a fricking compulsive, obsessive nut."

He laughed, because he has a similar personality type.

Ray moved to the United States from France, ran out of money, scraped around to get a job, and ended up building a multimillion-dollar business. He busted his ass, saved his money, and kept himself incredibly disciplined when it came to finances. He's obsessive, but in a different way from me.

Moderation is just not a word that's ever been in my vocabulary. I know moderation is a challenge for other people, too, because so often they will say, "I'm just going to drink on the weekends," or "I'm only going to have two drinks tonight," only for their resolve to go completely out the window. Drinking in moderation is a slippery slope, because alcohol lowers your inhibitions, making you more likely to loosen the standards you've set for yourself.

One of my good friends, Chris, who quit drinking a few months before I did, has an apt quote when it comes to moderation: "Triers are liars." The sentiment ties into

alcohol because we try to make bullsh*t pacts with ourselves to try to drink less—emphasis on *try*—only to fall
back to the spot where we started. When you decide to quit
drinking, tell yourself you aren't trying, you're doing, and
you shouldn't need to remind yourself of your standards.

To make the right move and go beyond trying, I felt I had
to commit to my decision 100 percent. In retrospect, it
was one of the best moves I've ever made in my life. It's
strange and wonderful to make a major life decision that
just feels right, without any doubt in your mind, and while
you might still feel fear, you shouldn't feel doubt. For me,
the decision was win-win. All I had to conquer was my
discomfort with breaking the habit.

MY HISTORY WITH ALCOHOL

As I've mentioned, my father was a serious alcoholic, so
alcohol has always had a presence in my life. I wonder
about his priorities: Were they his family? His career? His
health? No, ignoring his problems seemed like his number-
one priority, and drinking was his solution. Rather than
deal with the uncomfortable aspects of his life, my father
chose to numb his worries and fears indefinitely, and it
ruined him. Using alcohol to cope with self-doubt is something many people struggle with, but I didn't understand
why that's so dangerous until I was older.

Even though my father served as a warning light, showing me why I should avoid alcohol, I ended up drinking. As kids, we typically go in the direction opposite of where we're told to go, and my mom was strictly antialcohol. She'd have a glass of wine every once in a while, but fell into the category of people who could give up drinking entirely and never think twice about it. Even with my mom condemning alcohol, as a child, nobody ever said to me, "Look, your dad drank a lot. Both of your grandfathers struggled with alcohol. Alcohol is a risk in your family and you need to pump the brakes. Be careful."

Instead, I found myself drinking early. I had older friends who always had ways of getting alcohol, and usually, the kind of older guys who drink with kids four or five years younger than themselves aren't role models. Going as far back as the first time I got buzzed, when Dan and I stole his stepmom's wine coolers, I said, "I get it. I see why adults drink." As time progressed, I only drank more.

That's how this works for kids—they try something once, and then another time, and another—each instance seems minor on its own, but they add up. Eventually, they feel comfortable with something that had been completely foreign and frightening to them. Dan and I were best friends since first grade, so many of my early drinking experiences took place with him. Another memorable time at his house, his mom was out working while her boyfriend watched us.

He had a case of beer and said, "Hey, you guys are staying in. You can have a couple beers if you want."

We were around fourteen at the time. Naturally, Dan and I said, "Of course. We have beers all the time." That was completely untrue, but we didn't want to sound uncool.

Another time, Dan and I got our hands on some Zima with his younger brother Tim (who went on to star in the show *Detroiters* on Comedy Central) and our friend Terry. We slammed the Zimas and all got sick at the same time. Throwing up behind Dan's garage was in no way a good time, but it was still a bonding experience—something we went through together. It was one more drinking experience to add to the pile.

From there, my drinking grew heavier. On the last day before summer my junior year of high school, I got a fifth of Five O'Clock vodka and a gallon of lemonade to take to a party after school. My thought was, "I'm going to carry this around, and we'll all hang out and share it." I ended up drinking too much, and between the sugar and how intensely hot it was that day, I became hypoglycemic. I stumbled around completely inebriated—I couldn't walk, couldn't talk, and couldn't remember things later. I wasn't even eighteen at the time, and looking back, I think, "Damn, I had a problem, even then."

To give you an idea of what devious little a**holes my friends and I were in high school, here's an example of the things we would pull. One night, three cars worth of friends and I went to a party thrown by some guys who were also a bunch of a**holes. So, what did we do? We stole the keg—loaded it right into the trunk of my buddy's Ford Probe GT and couldn't even shut the hatch all the way. We bailed on the party and headed to the Burger King drive-through because a buddy who worked there would load us up with free Whoppers all the time.

So, there were about a dozen of us parked in the Burger King parking lot with a keg, chowing down on burgers, when the cops showed up. Back then, the police in the town where I grew up were a lot more lenient than police are nowadays. If they caught us with alcohol, they just brought us home, told our parents, and let them deal with us.

One of the cops brought me home and came into the house. He said, "Go get your mom. I want to talk to her."

Now, I was obviously intoxicated, so when I went to my mom's room and she asked, "Is there someone with you?"

I replied, "Yeah, this dickhead cop wants to—"

The officer grabbed me by the collar of my shirt and dragged me right back out to the cop car. He said, "You don't talk to me like that. You're taking a Breathalyzer."

My mom and the cop had it out because, realistically, he was being too rough, but before I talked back, he had been pretty cool. I think he'd planned to let me go until I opened my mouth. He gave me the Breathalyzer and I blew around a 0.20, which is more than twice the legal limit, plus I was only about sixteen years old.

The cop said, "Ma'am, your son has a problem. There's no way at his size and age he should be at this blood-alcohol level. I'm tempted to take him to the hospital."

My mom told him, "I'll watch him. He's fine."

I couldn't talk without slurring my words, but I could walk and remember everything, so I didn't need a doctor. The point is that, at a young age, I was already pushing the envelope. Splitting a case of beer with one other person was the norm, and while I never felt comfortable drinking and I driving, that doesn't mean I never did it. I walked a dangerous line.

As I got older and got a job, bought a nicer car, and so on,

I eased back on what I call "idiot drinking." Employment forced me out of the regular drinking crowd, but I worked at a bar, so I was still very much steeped in that lifestyle. Instead of drinking at happy hour, my coworkers and I would drink after our shifts until 7:00 a.m. I still drank more than I should have.

For ten years, the earliest I ever had to get to work was 4:00 p.m. Sometimes, I wouldn't have to go to work until 10:00 p.m. It's a drastically different lifestyle than most jobs, and it led me into all sorts of interesting situations. I lived with a friend named Jeff for six years during my twenties, and there's not a soul on Earth I've drank more beer with than him.

Right around the time Jeff and I were moving in together, I went out drinking hard one night. I must have passed out, because I woke up on a couch with blonde hair in my face. It was one of those mornings when you ask yourself, "How the hell did I get here? Are my kidneys still in?" At that phase in my life, hungover mornings when I woke up next to someone I'd just met weren't unusual, but this mystery person was sleeping in such a way that I couldn't see their face behind the blonde hair.

Nothing around me looked familiar. I wasn't at an ex-girlfriend's house or somewhere I'd been before. To make the situation weirder, I'd slept with my clothes on, so I just crept out of this strange apartment and called Jeff. This was before we used to party together, so I had to wonder whether Jeff thought, "Who the hell am I signing a lease with?" when he got my call.

I said, "Hey man, can you do me a favor? I woke up on some chick's couch and don't know where the hell I am."

"Look around. You see a street name?" Jeff asked.

I searched around and found a sign that said Village Green Apartments at Waterford, which fortunately was only fifteen minutes away from Jeff. He came to pick me up, and that's how he found out that this was the kind of person he was moving in with.

Later that day, I got a phone call from my friend Trinity. Trinity and I had always been friends and drinking buddies, but we'd never hooked up. She said, "Hey, where'd you go this morning?"

Still confused, I asked her, "What do you mean?"

"You were sleeping on my couch with me last night, and when I woke up, you were gone," she explained. "How'd you get home?"

She had recently moved into an apartment with a few friends, and I hadn't been there yet, which is why I didn't recognize the place. She told me I'd gotten a bit too messed up the night before and gotten in a fight, so she got me out of there. I felt relieved to solve the Mystery of the Blonde Hair, but waking up not knowing how or why I'd gotten somewhere was unnerving. Still, that's the kind of thing that happened from time to time, and the party didn't stop for six years.

My final story about drinking with my friends is a tragic one about a man named Jamie. Jamie and I first started hanging out during his senior year of high school, my junior year. He was the friend who would split a twenty-four-pack of Miller Lite Ice with me, a beer that had about 5.5 percent alcohol, which was a lot back then. Being high school students, we were stingy and would count how many beers we'd each had by keeping the tabs in our pockets.

I went to Mexico for spring break with Jamie and my other high school friends, and when Jamie blacked out, we left him on the beach. He woke up under the sun with the worst blistery sunburn covering his arms and forehead. I can't believe I laughed at him at the time. He must have been in terrible pain. Until I moved in with Jeff, there wasn't a person on Earth I drank more with than Jamie. I knew him for most of my life.

Flash forward nearly two decades, and Jamie decided to throw a party at his house. Our buddy Dan had moved away from our hometown, so when Dan came back to visit, Jamie wanted to get the old crew back together. By that point, many of us had eased off the alcohol, but Jamie started drinking hard in high school and had never let his foot off the gas. He began drinking early in the day before his party, and I can only speculate as to why. Maybe he felt nervous about seeing old friends or having a bunch of people at his house.

Whatever the reason, Jamie drank all day, got hammered, and passed out before guests arrived. Early in the evening, he woke up from his nap as people started to arrive, and he began pounding the drinks again. When more guests arrived, he was eager to show the guys his man cave in the basement. As he started walking down the stairs, he looked back to talk to his friends who were following him and he missed a step. Jamie fell, landed on his head, and cracked his skull, which caused severe internal bleeding in his brain. This ultimately led to his death in the hospital a couple days later. I wasn't there when the accident happened; the call came right as I was leaving my house to head to the party.

Two of my best friends, Dan and Terry, were there when Jamie slipped on the stairs and fell. At five foot ten and

270 pounds, Jamie was a big guy. He hit the ground hard and cracked his skull on the floor. Fifty people were at the hospital, waiting and hoping he'd wake up, when he died the next day. The doctor said he had so much alcohol in his system that they couldn't stop the hemorrhaging in time to save him.

Jamie's death was one of the first holy-sh*t moments for me when it came to drinking. It was the first time I thought, "All of us should quit drinking, guys. Seriously." Unfortunately, I think most of those friends still drink to this day, but even though we don't talk about it much, I know Jamie's death shook our group. It certainly scared me. What happened to Jamie could happen to any of us, especially as we get older and less coordinated, at any time. It's not as if he was driving drunk and swerved off the road; he was walking down the damn stairs.

This tragedy happened relatively recently, but I wanted to share the story at this point in the book because, even back in my twenties, I think I had a sense that the path my friends and I were on would end in disaster one day. Maybe not for all of us, and maybe not soon, but eventually the lifestyle we led would catch up to us.

Looking back at my years working in nightclubs, drunk people surrounded me all the time, and at a certain point,

I'd see the people I was serving and think, "God, I don't want to be like that fricking idiot." Working at the clubs helped me see alcohol in a different, less glamorous light.

I scaled back my drinking and eventually met my wife, after which I left the nightclub scene. Moving into a corporate job and working from 8:00 a.m. to 7:00 p.m. helped me cut down on the alcohol even more, but I still drank. I suddenly found myself in the happy-hour, grab-a-beer-after-work crowd, and I'd still drink excessively at concerts, football games, and vacations. Finally, body-building forced me to decide: Do I want to look great and win competitions, or do I want to get drunk?

My long history with alcohol demonstrates that I didn't go from getting drunk every night to not drinking at all. Cutting down on alcohol happened gradually over the years, from my binge-drinking phase to drinking wine with dinner. When I decided to quit, I still drank a not-insignificant amount every day. What was the next step in this natural progression? Cutting out alcohol entirely.

REGULAR DRINKING VERSUS BINGE DRINKING: KNOW THE DIFFERENCE

The difference between regular drinking and binge drinking is somewhere between one drink and blacking out.

Yes, that range is intentionally dramatic. In my opinion, anywhere within that range is potentially the danger zone, which ties into my belief that even one drink isn't going to work if you have a problem.

When alcohol is all around us, it's tough to say no—and it's everywhere. Even at my son's indoor soccer practice, they serve beer, and all the dads sit around drinking. The more you're exposed to alcohol, the more you're going to drink. I've seen it happen before. Someone will drink in social situations two or three times a week. At first, they'll stick to only two or three drinks, but over time, they'll creep up to three or four, then four or five. Before they know it, they're drinking five drinks five nights a week.

Nobody becomes an alcoholic overnight. Becoming an excessive drinker is a gradual process, which is exactly the reason why it can be hard to catch. The build-up happens when you say, "Just one more drink," a phrase that sounds harmless on its own, but that becomes a problem when you've already said it five times before. Of course, many people never develop a problem, but for the people who have a propensity for alcohol abuse, bingeing starts with that first drink.

The tough part about binge drinking is that, frankly, it can be a lot of fun. Many of my funniest experiences happened while binge drinking. However, I've realized now that it wasn't the alcohol making those experiences fun; it was the atmosphere and my connection with other people. When I worked in nightclubs, I met some cool, hilarious people, and the fact that they drank wasn't what made them good company.

I worked at a nightclub called Clutch Cargo's in downtown Pontiac, Michigan, and every year, the staff would go on a three-day canoe trip together. My roommate Jeff and I were invited to the trip the first year I worked there and were told it was a couples' trip. Both of our girlfriends at the time were a bit bossy—we would joke and call them fun governors. We decided to leave them behind so we could do what we wanted and not have anyone telling us to stop. We could canoe together, drink, and carry on.

Jeff and I went on the trip that year with about fourteen other people and were the only two guys in a canoe together; everyone else was there as a couple. The two of us going without girlfriends opened the trip up to other noncouples and the number of people attending skyrocketed over the years. The biggest turnout for this trip was about sixty-five people, and the coolest part about this group was the diversity among us. There were people who were nineteen years old and people who were forty-five, people who were black, white, gay, tattooed, mohawked,

preppy—you name it. They nicknamed Jeff and me Barbie
and Ken, and we had a blast. You couldn't ask for a better
group of people. I really loved all those guys.

I went on this trip for about ten years, so I saw its full
evolution. I ended up bringing girlfriends, and my wife
even joined me on one of the later trips. The rule was that
Jeff and I always canoed together, and the one thing that
stayed consistent about these canoe trips is that they were
always absolute sh*t shows. Everybody would get in their
canoes and drink all day long. Jeff and I went through a
couple cases of beer one year. After cracking open our
first beer at 8:00 a.m., we spent the whole day drifting
down the river. We wouldn't even paddle most of the time
because we were too busy joking and drinking. We'd all
barrel down the river like a Mötley Crüe show, with thirty
canoes blocking the whole river, all decorated with crazy
signs. By the time we came in wasted at nighttime, we'd
have lost some paddles and made the canoe company
livid, but it was such a fun trip.

I believe, however, that everyone on the trip could've had
the same fun without drinking. I think that because when
I see some of these people years later, we share the same
gut-wrenching laughs without alcohol. The context of the
trip might've been different without drinking, but I know
that group of people would've still been mooning each

other, blasting each other with squirt guns, and whipping grapes at each other, regardless.

There are times when alcohol forces the fun, like the time I mentioned when I was drinking beer in my buddy's garage, but some situations are just not salvageable, even with your standards lowered by alcohol. It's so easy to associate the genuinely good old times with drinking, too, but we don't need the alcohol to make those memories. The people, the atmosphere, and the mindset are all there whether you drink or not.

WHEN THE PARTY LOSES ITS LUSTER

At the height of my drinking, I always loved a good time. Now that I don't drink at all, I still always love a good time. Enjoying the fun associated with drinking has never changed for me. I simply realized I could take alcohol out of the equation. Before that realization, quitting was out of the question. Even the idea of not drinking seemed f**king crazy to me. Making the commitment to never drink again would've scared me more than getting married, and I bet a lot of other people feel that way too.

Don't believe it? When people get married, they're essentially saying, "I'm only going to be with this one person for the rest of my life." Ask them to give up alcohol forever, and you might hear, "Forever? I don't know about that..." When you break it down, giving up alcohol is simpler than many other commitments. You're just not doing something anymore. There are, of course, many other reasons that make quitting hard, but from a purely mechanical standpoint, removing alcohol is doing less. Your default state of being is not drinking alcohol. Compare it to the commitment of going to the gym every day. It takes more effort to go to the gym than to not go. You need to actively do something to make it happen. Not so with removing alcohol.

The idea of quitting used to be crazy to me, but that lifestyle felt old once I met my wife and had a family. Suddenly, I had other things to focus on and other sources of joy in my life. My old lifestyle of drinking and partying felt like false fulfillment in comparison. I felt even more strongly about my new life when my wife and I had our daughter. Having a little girl in and of itself softened me up, but it had also been four years since we had our son. In that time, I matured and developed a deeper appreciation for my role in my children's lives.

I started thinking less about me and more about my kids. Everything I didn't like about my childhood, I now had the opportunity to change for them. I could share knowledge with them. I could help them discover their hobbies and passions. I could do all the things that my parents may not have been able to do for me. However, to do these things for my children, I needed to make sure there was enough of me to give. I wouldn't let alcohol keep me from being around, as it had with my father.

In thinking about my children, my father, and alcohol, I became more aware of my drinking habits. I didn't drink too often when my kids were very young, but my wife and I would still go out on the boat and have a few beers, or go on a couples' vacation and drink excessively. The instances when I drank too much became relatively rare, but they still happened.

MY TURNING POINT

I can pinpoint one moment that I'd call the ultimate turning point for me, a moment that still brings a tear to my eye. It was summertime, and my wife and I had some of her friends over. We went out on the boat, hung out, and drank. The friends were a couple we hadn't seen in a while, which made the evening a little uncomfortable, and they were spending the night. If they had left earlier in the evening, I probably would've stopped drinking, but instead I over indulged.

As I stumbled around the house, I tripped on one of the

kids' toys and made a loud clatter. I'd definitely had too much to drink. The loud noise I made caused my son to wake up and come downstairs, only for him to find me trying to use the wall to get back up from the spill I'd just taken in the family room. What he saw completely freaked him out: the sight of me struggling to get back up off the ground.

He burst into hysterical tears and asked, "What's wrong with Dad?"

I told him, "Go back upstairs," but he noticed I was slurring my words and that something was wrong with me.

The next day, I didn't remember what happened until my wife and her friends mentioned it. In that moment, I didn't want to deal with reality, so I ignored what had happened and shoved any concerns to the back of my mind. However, I couldn't shut out that incident forever. I thought about it. I thought about it a lot, and the more I thought about my actions, the more it struck a nerve. I'd done some things that weren't very nice over the years while drinking—hurting people's feelings, getting into fights, going home with girls and never calling. I'd never felt especially bad about those things, but when I saw my son more upset than I'd ever seen him in his life, the loving father in me had some serious things to say to binge-drinking me: "Who the f**k do you think you are, making my son upset?"

I was pissed at myself. If some other adult had made my son that upset, I'd have probably knocked them out, but there I was making him cry. There's nothing I care about more than my children. Even thinking about the incident today hits home and deeply bothers me, because the last thing I want is for my children to grow up in a household like my father's. I saw my father drunk many times, and he was an angry drunk. I remembered the fear that had instilled itself in me as a little kid and knew that I absolutely could not do that to my kids. They didn't deserve that—no kid deserves that.

AN ACCEPTABLE EXCUSE

When I sat down and thought about the incident with my son, it was the first time I decided I wanted to quit drinking. Alcohol had lost its appeal. In those early days, I had a glass of wine or two with my wife, or if we were going out on the boat or some other place, I would usually be drinking. As time went on, the biggest problem I had was not having a solid excuse for not drinking.

In my opinion, pride and ego are good for you, but they got in my way by saying, "I don't want to quit because the only people who quit are people who have a problem." I didn't want people to think I'd hit rock bottom by losing my job or getting a DUI. I pictured the guy riding his bike because he'd lost his driver's license—I wasn't one of those people and didn't want to associate myself with them.

That thought right there—the worry of being called a loser or coming off as out-of-control—keeps a lot of people from quitting. I knew that if I told people I'd quit because I wanted to improve myself, they'd wonder what I wasn't telling them.

I even told one of my best friends, who quit drinking twenty years ago, and he asked, "What really happened?"

I said, "What do you mean?"

He replied, "What happened? People don't just quit drinking." He was in Alcoholics Anonymous and sponsored a lot of people, so from his perspective, there had to be an incident like a DUI that made me want to quit.

When I gave him the long answer about wanting to improve myself, his response was essentially, "Huh."

My friend hadn't heard that reason for quitting before, and his response made me realize something. To make my decision less of a blow to my pride and easier for other people to swallow, I needed an excuse. When I thought about it, the answer was right in front of my eyes: my father.

At the time, my father was still alive, but he had alcohol-induced dementia. He spoke with a slur and couldn't even remember that he drank or smoked. He died at only sixty-two years old on September 17, 2015, at one in the afternoon. I love my family and want to spend as much time as I can with them. The goals I want to accomplish take time, and I want to be around to have grandchildren. None of that can happen if I become incoherent at sixty-two years old.

Toward the end, before my father died, I decided that his death would be my excuse to quit drinking. I imagined that if someone asked me, "Why don't you drink?" I would reply with, "My dad had a drinking problem that ultimately killed him, so I decided to give up alcohol when he died," and it would be a perfectly reasonable answer. No one would question it. It was a reason I'd even be comfortable telling a stranger.

PULLING THE TRIGGER

At the time, I had no idea how much longer my father would live. The doctor had told us six months, and he ended up living six years. In any case, I had a little time before I had to make good on my commitment to myself. Around that time, I was working on a merger between one of my companies and a large conglomerate and was in Las Vegas when I got the call. My stepmom and I would text each other frequently, so I knew his death was coming any day.

When he died, I remembered my decision, but I realized I wasn't ready to quit drinking quite yet. I still wanted to quit sometime, just not then. I had so much on my plate between my family and this significant business merger, and I used that as an excuse to postpone my promise to myself. It was easier to stick to my status quo of sitting down with work in the evenings and throwing back a couple drinks. In hindsight, that style of working was a poor process.

If you'd asked me whether it's easier to get work done in the evening with a drink or two, I would have said yes. Without a doubt, I got work done, but was it my best work? Definitely not. Sometimes, we think we have a better grip on things than we do, and when we look back at our past actions, we say, "I can't believe I ever thought that way." Drinking while working was one of those times for me. Now that I don't drink, I see how much more productive I am without the alcohol.

I heard an adage from my wife's old boss that sums up the reality of my drinking-and-working habit nicely: "Draft your emails when you're drinking; edit and send them when you're sober." It might be easier to dig into emotions with a buzz, but it's also easier to make mistakes. To an extent, I was in denial about the effect drinking had on my work, which made quitting seem less urgent.

Months passed, until the day came when I did a serious self-assessment. I couldn't remember the last day I'd spent without a drink. Not a single day without at least one glass of wine. Like I mentioned earlier in the chapter, it's easy to think a single drink is no big deal, but when you don't go a day without that drink, it's a red flag. I wondered if I could go for a day without drinking. A week? A month? I honestly didn't know the answer, because I had never explicitly tried before.

A month before the anniversary of my father's death, I told my wife, "I think I'm ready to stop drinking, but I need your support. I need you all-in when it comes to never making me feel like a dick for not drinking, never tempting me, and never trying to pressure me into having a glass of wine. I need that commitment from you before I can even consider doing this."

My wife is amazing, and said, "Of course. I support you."

She and I have had a lot of fun times drinking, so she probably wishes things were different, but she is incredibly supportive. We used to share a bottle of wine in the evenings or go to a restaurant to split an appetizer, get drinks, and catch up. We still do those things, but I order a Diet Coke instead.

Checking in with each other and making sure the other person is still having a good time is another practice that has helped our relationship. I want her to feel comfortable having her glass of wine around me, because when you're drinking and getting buzzed, but the person you're with isn't, it can make you feel guilty. The person who isn't drinking doesn't feel as silly as you, and you might worry they won't find you funny. This hasn't been a problem with my wife because she almost never drinks enough to get tipsy, but if you're with someone who likes to get buzzed, be aware of how they might be feeling.

Labor Day was coming up when my wife and I had one of our check-ins. Every year for Labor Day, her aunt and uncle come to visit from Friday to Monday. They ride Harleys, go to Sturgis Bike Week, and have a tight-knit relationship with their adult children. Generally, they're just some of the coolest, most laid-back, nonjudgmental people I know. We hang out by the lake when they come to visit, and even though no one ever gets drunk, beers start cracking open at 10:00 a.m. Then we spend the day going out on the boat, hanging by the pool, and fishing. When the sun goes down, we pull out the grill and start up the bonfire.

They came to visit shortly after I decided to quit drinking but before I'd pulled the trigger. I didn't want to be a Debbie Downer for the weekend, knowing that they roll into town with four coolers of beer. That weekend, we were also going to the wedding of a good friend who loves to drink and party, so I knew his wedding would be a wild time.

I thought about these events and said to my wife, "After this weekend, I'm done drinking." Finally, the timing felt right.

On Friday, I tore it up with my wife's aunt and uncle on the lake. Saturday, we went to the wedding. Sunday, we drank wine on the boat. When you drink three days in a row, you feel disgusting, like you've been stuck in a Mexican prison for a week, but feeling like garbage made those first days of quitting easier. When my wife's aunt and uncle left our house on Monday, my life without alcohol officially started.

I didn't give up drinking because I was an alcoholic or

because I found God, and I want to reiterate that you don't need to experience an inciting event in order to quit either. For me, my main "why" came down to performing a life assessment and realizing the potential dangers of alcohol outweighed the benefits. The choice almost felt like a business decision, as though I were changing the direction of my company or making an investment. The only difference was that the investment was me.

Think about your life and ask yourself, "Is drinking going to yield me the return I want? Is it going to return *any* yield? Or, is it more likely to bring me a loss?" Personally, there were too many terrible situations that could happen while I was drinking. I could do something stupid that caused my wife to leave me. Losing her and my kids was a potential life's-over-for-good, stuck-in-Loserville, drinking-every-day scenario. There'd be no coming back from that downfall. Worse than them deciding to leave, what if my family died in a car accident? I saw that alcohol would only bring me losses, so I pulled the trigger and cut it from my life. There was no having one drink on the weekends—I quit, full stop, and I'm not going back.

Even if something tragic had happened that was out of my control, if I was in the habit of drinking a bottle of wine a night, what would happen then? Would I stop drinking? No, I'd most likely start drinking two bottles of wine a night. When you're in a vulnerable place and relying on drugs or alcohol, only one bad thing has to happen in order for you to never recover.

On the other hand, when you work on improving yourself and living a satisfying life, those positives compound upon themselves as well. When you're happier, you have more energy and focus to create, to pursue your goals, and to learn. We think that a new car, a tropical vacation, or a fancy cocktail will make us happy, but they don't. Those things might bring you momentary joy, but they're a flash in the pan. True happiness is found in self-growth and accomplishment, which rise to full power when you quit drinking.

Life is amazing, but it's also fragile when you're careless. It's up to you to take control of your decisions rather than relinquish them to alcohol, and that starts with looking at your life and figuring out the "why" behind your choice to quit.

CHAPTER FOUR

HOW I QUIT

The hardest part of quitting for me was the word "forever." Generally speaking, I don't want most things to last forever. It took me a long time before I felt comfortable and happy with the concept of being married forever. Then when I had children, I had another moment of growth when I realized, "These are my kids, forever." Growing older chipped away at the intimidation of long-term commitment—especially positive commitment.

While family deserves that level of commitment, nothing else in my life qualifies for forever. That's not to say other aspects of life are disposable, but I've owned about eight cars over the past decade, for example. I never had the cars all at one time—I'd get tired of a car and trade it in for a different model. The point is that something like owning a car is a relatively fleeting commitment.

I take commitment incredibly seriously. Naturally, it requires a lot of consideration before I make a decision. When I commit to a goal, I'm going to keep it, so if I say I'm quitting alcohol forever, I'll never drink again. I value discipline and recognize that it's perhaps the most important quality you can have for reaching your goals. In my personal life, I have achieved just about everything I set out to do, and this commitment would be no different. In business, I've had investors buy into my company simply because they know my personality, know I'm disciplined, and know that nothing's going to stop me—I'm relentless.

When I decided to quit drinking, I realized the next step was to let people know. In my experience, publicizing your goals is one of the most important things you can do to help you stay committed. Naturally, we don't want to disappoint the people around us or admit defeat. It's embarrassing to have to tell someone you didn't reach your goal. Use that to your advantage. I'm sure you have met someone who started doing CrossFit or became vegan—they don't miss an opportunity to announce their goals to the world. In all seriousness, voicing your goals is one of the most important steps to achieving them. If you are scared to tell someone your goals, it's probably because you don't truly believe you can accomplish them.

Whether you're running a 5K, writing a book, or quitting

drinking, tell every person you know—you'll be far more likely to hold yourself accountable. Those people will be there to remind you of your promises, and by telling them early on in the process, you'll get the discomfort of breaking the news out of the way. You won't have to worry about how or when to bring up the fact that you're giving up alcohol if you're upfront about it from the very beginning.

Taking on a long-term, significant goal excited me, because the harder the challenge, the more it's going to hold my attention. Giving up alcohol forever is in a different league than, say, pledging to not eat cereal at night. Cutting out cereal might last eighteen days or so before I say, "F**k it, eat a bowl of cereal. Who cares?" Giving up alcohol is bigger—it qualifies as a major lifestyle change. I have become more compassionate to vegans, because giving up all animal products is a major change, on par with quitting alcohol, but even harder. Vegans need to carefully monitor what they consume and seek out alternatives to common foods—it involves a lot of extra effort. Quitting alcohol is simply NOT consuming something you don't need in your life.

THE THIRTY-DAY HURDLE

As I discussed in the previous chapter, when I quit, I had just made it through a long summer of hanging out at the lake, eating garbage, and traveling. It was the time of year I call "the Labor Day Riot," when people have their last hurrah of the summer before cleaning up their act to get the kids back to school and lightening up their social schedule.

I felt mentally prepared to take time off drinking anyway. However, the next thirty days I had planned weren't what you'd call conducive to an alcohol-free lifestyle. My work schedule was packed: I had a five-day business trip to Las Vegas coming up, a trip to Chicago with the Detroit Lions, and an Adele concert—all situations where I'd usually consume alcohol.

I knew I had a ton of meetings lined up in Vegas where potential customers would be drinking, and I had no delusions about it—not drinking would be uncomfortable. After all, if there's any place where drinking excessively is expected, it's Vegas. In the past, I had taken trips to Vegas where my friends and I arrived at the hotel, went out partying, passed out, woke up, and partied again. I didn't even gamble. One time when I visited Vegas for four days, I had flown in at night and flown out on the red-eye, without ever going outside or seeing daylight, and now I planned to not drink at all.

The Chicago trip would be equally challenging. The friend

joining me works with the Detroit Lions, so I knew I'd be hanging out with the team, going to dinners, and attending events with open bars. No doubt, it would be awkward to drink a Diet Coke or nothing at all at a champagne reception, but I felt determined and confident about the challenge.

One trick to meeting your goals is to acknowledge your small victories. For example, if you're trying to eat less sugar and you successfully turn down the mini donuts sitting out at your workplace every day, you'll likely feel proud of yourself. Little wins like that build your confidence and help you hold onto whatever goal you've set. For me, not drinking in Vegas for five days would be one of those confidence-boosting wins. I knew if I had the willpower to avoid drinking there, I'd come home with the mindset of a badass. I could stare down any future challenge and simply say, "Bring it."

People knew me as a drinker, so before my first trip, I prepared to answer their questions. I asked myself, "What's the best thing to do in an awkward situation?" That's when I decided I needed a story. If you imagine breaking your foot or getting a black eye, everybody who sees you wants to know what happened. Maybe you fell, or maybe you got in a bar fight, but you're a professional and don't want to admit it. You need to be prepared for people to ask.

My wife once got a black eye after passing out from being dehydrated. She woke up in the middle of the night, and she got out of bed to use the restroom. All of a sudden, I heard a loud thud. I thought someone was breaking into our house and ran out to find her with her face all bloodied up. For a minute, I thought someone had come in and attacked her, but she had actually fainted and hit her head on the sink. She was fine after that, but sported a black eye for a few weeks.

Even a decade after this had happened, one of her friends asked her, "What happened that night? It's been a long time, you can tell me." Everyone wants to know "the real story." Being at a social event without a drink in hand, especially when people know you as a drinker, is a lot like having a black eye.

I already had the one excuse for quitting—that my dad had died from drinking—that I could use without trying to explain my quest for self-improvement, but I wanted something a little less heavy to tell work acquaintances. It had to be a short-and-sweet story that wouldn't make people uncomfortable or require many follow-up questions. I thought about my lifestyle and what kind of reason would make sense for me, and decided on something completely innocuous but difficult to argue against: "I'm doing a month-long, post-Labor Day detox."

The reason worked like a charm. I've always been concerned about fitness and in above-average shape, so when I told people, "I'm doing a personal cleanup: quit drinking, improving the diet, waking up in the morning and hitting the gym," it made sense. It fit with their notion of who I am as a person. The most common response I received when people asked why I wasn't drinking and heard my answer was, "Oh, cool." Not having to answer questions made the situation less stressful for me.

It's hard for people to argue against a reason like "I'm doing a personal cleanup" when they're in worse shape than you and they go to the gym less often than you. People don't want to talk about areas where they're lacking in comparison, and I think that tendency worked to my advantage.

I made it through those trips to Vegas and Chicago without cracking, but that's not to say it didn't test my will. Vegas turned out to be the easier trip of the two, mainly because I was around people in the fitness industry who had to get up early for business meetings and go to competitions, so nobody drank excessively.

The most trying moment for me was in Chicago, when my friend and I were hanging out with a dynamic group for dinner. Multimillionaires, successful business owners, and retired NFL players—people who, as an entrepreneur, I wanted to play ball with—surrounded me. I looked at some of these people and thought, "Holy sh*t! I have this guy's business card now, and we're hanging out laughing? Don't blow it." It was tempting to try to go with the flow rather than stand out as the awkward guy who wasn't ordering a drink.

When the moment came for the drinks to start flowing, I didn't know what to do. These were people I wanted to impress, and I knew by refusing drinks, I'd stand out as weird instead of fitting right in. Still, I stuck to my guns. When I told them, "No thanks, I'm good," it definitely raised a few eyebrows. Everyone was dressed to the nines and drinking expensive wine—it was the kind of situation where people don't normally turn down the generous offerings.

When I told them I was doing a thirty-day detox, their reactions surprised me. People were positive and respectful. Especially the retired athletes—those guys all got it. At some point, they had to do the same thing to be more competitive on the field. They commended me on my discipline. I had been so anxious about going against the status quo that it never occurred to me that the reception I received might be the opposite of what I feared. The rest of the night was perfect, and drinking was never in the front of my mind again.

MAPPING OUT YOUR FIRST THIRTY DAYS

My easy excuse helped me a great deal in circumventing those busy first thirty days. Equally important was mapping out a plan. Why focus on thirty days? Thirty days is long enough to form new habits and share your decision with your inner circle, but short enough that you're aware of any big events coming up and can think about your plan day by day. It really can be a day-by-day scenario. You can't avoid all social situations and turn into a hermit. If you do, I think you will crack and feel like quitting alcohol has affected your happiness adversely, when really you affected your happiness by limiting your social situations.

I approached my strategy to quit drinking much like I'd approach my nutrition plan when I was bodybuilding and training for a competition. With my nutrition plan, I'd write out all the food I intended to eat in a week. I knew that on Friday, meal five at 7:00 p.m., I'd be eating six ounces of steak and a cup of broccoli. I'd map out every meal and prep all my food in advance so I'd have it ready. The same approach worked for my training schedule. I knew exactly what I was doing for every workout.

When it comes to drinking, think about your next thirty days and answer these questions:

- What events will you be attending?
- Where and when can you expect to be in a social situation involving alcohol?
- What can you do to distract yourself from not drinking?
- What will your story be when people ask why you're not drinking?
- What will you drink instead of alcohol?
- What's after the first thirty days?
- Who will support your decision?
- Who might resist your decision?

Figuring out how to deal with social situations will take a lot of the stress out of not drinking. Know what you're going to drink when you go out with friends. Diet Coke? Water? An alcohol-free cocktail? Don't give anyone the chance to say, "Come on, just have one beer," by taking too long to decide what to order. Be decisive and confident, and no one will challenge you. It's also okay to just say, "No, thank you," when offered a drink. It is totally fine to not have a beverage in your hand.

I treated my first thirty days without alcohol like a trial period where I could figure out how to handle social situations, get my story straight, come up with a long-term strategy, and, most of all, develop the level of confidence to be successful. Maintaining my decision indefinitely would be difficult, but first, I just had to get through those thirty days. Focusing on the first thirty days helped me feel less overwhelmed by my commitment. I could look at every one of those days and come up with a plan of attack.

Determined to take it one day at a time, I forced myself to go to the gym every morning. Those kind of habits—working out, eating a healthy meal, reading a book—helped me feel good about myself. When you feel good about yourself, it's easier to maintain self-control over habits that you think will make you feel better but are bad for you.

Overall, I lived a super healthy lifestyle those first thirty days and beyond, to the point that my wife asked me around day ninety if I had gotten Botox or a facial treatment. She told me I looked younger and healthier. I felt better, too. By the end of that first month, it seemed cutting out alcohol and living a less-toxic life had almost no downsides.

THE NEXT THIRTY DAYS

My first thirty days without alcohol, with all of the social events I had planned, were a formidable challenge. At the same time, being so busy helped the days pass quickly. Staying occupied allowed me to run from the full weight of my decision for a bit, in that I didn't slow down enough to get hung up on my choices.

The next thirty days were a different challenge entirely. I had far fewer social obligations to fulfill, but I still had to deal with myself. I suddenly had plenty of time to look in the mirror and grapple with my decision in private. The exciting honeymoon phase, when the challenge was new and exhilarating, had passed, and what was left felt much more *blah*. I had to decide how to stay strong in my decision in the absence of excitement.

As international sales expert Grant Cardone put it, "If you want to meet the devil, just leave some white space on your calendar." I found this quote to be especially true when trying to give up drinking. I kept busy by setting new fitness goals, structuring my day more clearly, focusing on my two businesses, and making quality evening family time a priority. An average day looked like this:

6 a.m.—Wake up, put coffee on, get the kids up and eating breakfast.

7 a.m.—Hit the gym and see the family off to school and work.

8 a.m.—Get dressed and settle in to my home office.

9 a.m.—Start working.

Noon—Eat lunch and browse the news or check social media.

1 p.m.—Get back to work.

4 p.m.—Spend time with my kids after school.

5 p.m.—Sit down to work again (in the past, this is when I'd usually grab my first drink).

7 p.m.—Eat dinner and enjoy some family time.

9 p.m.—Get back to work.

11 p.m.—Unwind with some TV or a book.

Midnight—Go to sleep.

In my early days of quitting, I ran from the beast, so to speak, and made sure I kept busy. When you're focused so hard on something productive, you don't have time to entertain bad ideas, which for me was drinking. Throwing myself into work paid off. From a revenue standpoint, my first thirty days off drinking was the best month one of my companies ever had. The success caught my attention. For the first time, I thought, "Holy sh*t, not drinking could have some real positive outcomes." Until you remove alcohol from your life, you really have no clue how the productivity in your life can increase in all areas.

As the days passed without alcohol, my mind felt sharper and I had a surge of new creativity, as though I'd had two miles of visibility and that distance had suddenly expanded to five. I spent about sixty hours a week on the businesses I was building. I rebranded and laid out a whole new roadmap for that company. I'll admit, there were even a couple moments when I looked at my work and thought, "Damn, I really came up with that?" I patted myself on the back a bit because I knew my improved work output was the result of my brain being wide awake and free of alcohol. Problem solving became a faster process. Back when I drank, I may have had ideas that I was too lazy to write down or too distracted to see through. However, I'd outgrown those habits and now strived to be the kind of person who works so hard that he needs a thirty-hour day and a four-hundred-day year to squeeze it all in.

There have been times when the weekend has actually annoyed me, because everyone else in business moves so slowly on the weekend. But, we all need balance. Now I've shifted my schedule so that I unplug from Saturday afternoon to Sunday evening. When eight o'clock rolls around on Sunday night, I'm back to being a crazy man. It's not a lifestyle for everyone, but I love putting my shoulder to the grindstone and seeing my businesses grow as a result. If you're an entrepreneurial, results-driven person, I'm sure you can relate. Being able to provide a lifestyle and an example for my kids that I never had was a top priority.

DO WHAT IT TAKES TO GET THROUGH THE DAY

It may be simple, but one of the most effective habits that helped me quit drinking was finding something new to drink. Many people who fall into the heavier or binge-drinking category are fast drinkers. I'm talking about the guy who finishes his beer while the rest of his group is only halfway through theirs. I fit that description. No matter where I am, no matter what I'm drinking, if there's a drink in my hand, it's going to be gone quickly. Even today, if I'm out to dinner or in any social situation, I'm the guy who always needs a refill on my Diet Coke or LaCroix.

When I go out for lunch and order a Diet Coke, I easily go through three or four refills, so you can imagine what I was like when I drank beer. For whatever reason, I'm thirsty all the time, and when I cut out alcohol, I knew my thirst wouldn't magically cease to exist. The other side of the coin that I knew would be challenging was losing the act of fixing a drink. I used to enjoy mixing liquors or picking out wine varietals and had to somehow preserve that element of interest.

I said to myself, "If picking out wines is interesting, maybe water can be the same." Every time I went to the store, I bought a different kind of bottled water: spring water, artesian water, sparkling water, flavored water. It was a full-blown distraction mission to find something new to drink in the evenings when I would typically drink alcohol. Guess what? It worked.

I finally landed on a brand of seltzer water called LaCroix and tried every variety they offered. They are a Detroit-based company, which made me like them even more. After trying every flavor, I figured out I liked passion fruit the best. Now, I drink four to six cans a night. The point I'm trying to make is that, while obsessing over bottled water may sound crazy, I did whatever I could not to drink or think about drinking at a time when I was so accustomed to having a cocktail in hand. Some nights, in the beginning, I admittedly even smoked a couple cigarettes, which I hadn't done in years.

If you're removing a daily habit, you need to fill that space with something else, and my one goal was to find a new habit that wasn't as bad as drinking. I found it also helped to give myself rewards that I considered indulgences. I'm not a huge dessert eater, but during those early days of quitting, I told myself, "I didn't drink five-hundred calories in alcohol tonight, so to hell with it, I'm going to have some cheesecake or ice cream." I knew I'd be going to the gym in the morning, so eating dessert wasn't a decision I felt too guilty about—you don't want to pick up a habit that will hurt your self-esteem like overeating, but I had fun with it. I'd take my kids out for ice cream or, like with my water sampling, pick out a different flavored pint of some premium cold treat each time I went to the grocery store: salted caramel, cheesecake brownie, mint chip, and on and on.

At one point, I ate half a pint of ice cream every night after dinner, and it helped me get through those rough early days. When I felt more comfortable without alcohol, I said to myself, "All right, dude. You don't need ice cream every night. That's not the guy you are," and I reined in the habit. Changing my habits had to occur in progressive steps in order for it to stick, and what that meant for me was snacking a bit more and having a little treat instead of a drink.

Don't quit drinking and start shooting heroin, obviously, but know that it's okay to indulge in a guilty pleasure if it will help you quit. The important part is to go into a new habit with an exit plan. If I was going to eat chips, I was also going to tell myself that I was a disgusting POS for doing it every night, and I would pick a day to stop with the junk. It sounds harsh, but for any bad habit you try to quit, it can actually help to focus on the negatives. I told myself what I was doing was stupid, gross, and that it made me a loser. Some people thrive only on positive reinforcement, but shaming myself worked for the way my mind is wired.

You do what you have to do, whether that's picking up a guilty habit, obsessing over a benign subject, or calling yourself names. Find whatever you have to do to get through the day and those first thirty, sixty, and ninety alcohol-free days will be so much more bearable. Be unstoppable.

FIND YOUR IRONCLAD MOTIVATION

My number-one key takeaway is that, in order to successfully quit, you need to be motivated. You can't read a book and say, "That sounds like a good idea. I think I'll try to quit"—your motivation has to come from a deeper place. Along the same lines, no one else can make you motivated if you don't truly want to quit—not your spouse, your friends, your children, or your therapist—just you.

It's my hope that this book can help you see the places in your life where you have much to gain by removing alcohol, as well as assuage any fears that your social life will suffer without drinking. The first thirty days will be challenging, but if you follow a strict roadmap with limited white space on your calendar, your transition should be easier. Commit to maintaining your social life—not dodging events—waking up early, and trying new activities.

When it comes time to go to that first social event after you quit drinking, go into it with a plan. Know what your story will be when someone inevitably questions your choices. Growing up, I was always a troublemaker, so I had a lot of practice coming up with excuses and stories. For other people, not being completely honest can be a little tougher. The way I see it, if you have to tell some bullsh*t to change your life in a way that doesn't even affect other people's lives, you have to do it.

You aren't maliciously lying; having a story is a strategy, and it's important for you as a person to feel comfortable in moving forward with your goal. Keep your story tight, keep it easy to tell, and do what you have to do to free yourself from alcohol.

CHAPTER FIVE

HOW YOU CAN QUIT, TOO

Motivation is critical to quitting, so ask yourself how badly you want to give up drinking. Are you serious about the commitment or is it just an idea you'd like to try? How much thought have you given to the decision? In general, we tend to be more externally focused on things like our smartphones, television, the news, politics, and other distractions. We have a million things in our day-to-day lives that steal our attention and keep our brains too busy for introspection. It's easy to miss potential points of self-improvement, but a life-altering change like giving up alcohol requires you to gain perspective on your life and take some time to focus on yourself.

If, after some quality introspection, you decide you are

motivated—great. The next step is asking yourself, "Why?" Your reason for quitting will typically be something in your life that you're not willing to compromise, like your future health, your relationships, or your career trajectory. It's no coincidence that I made the decision to quit during a time in my life when I was making a conscious effort to look inward. I spent more time reading and less time watching television.

I asked why for everything about myself and sought hard reasons: Why did I drink? Why did I feel the need to dress a certain way? Why did I skip the gym when I knew I should go? Why did I eat foods I shouldn't eat? Why did I keep a toxic person in my life longer than I should have? The good thing about quitting alcohol is that there are no wrong reasons to quit.

IT'S YOUR FAULT, AND THAT'S OKAY

The other side to this process is not accepting bullsh*t answers from yourself. Asking difficult questions about your life and choices is uncomfortable, but you need to keep it real if you want to make progress. Bullsh*t answers won't get you anywhere. By lying to yourself, all you'd be doing is ignoring the problem and keeping yourself in a prison of ignorance for that much longer. Your time is too important to waste in that way.

Ask yourself the hard questions, and then follow up with a deeper dig. Did you do something out of insecurity? Neediness? Laziness? Fear? When we look into our core and stop blaming the world for our problems, it's like turning on the lights in the attic. You look at what's revealed, and ask yourself, "All these things are up here?" Sift through the little truths you discover—get rid of the negatives and focus on making the positives even better.

You've likely heard "a glass of wine a day is healthy," but for most people who say this, I believe it's just an excuse to have a drink. A shot of apple cider vinegar is also healthy, but you don't see most of that same crowd drinking one of those every night with their glass of wine. I'm reminded of a time I saw an article in a fitness magazine about how looking at photos of attractive women is good for men's heart health. The article went on to explain that looking at images of attractive women increased men's heart rate, which had a positive cardiovascular effect. I happened to be with my father-in-law at the time, who is a flirtatious older French gentleman—the kind of guy who will put his arm around your girlfriend and offer her a drink in a totally innocent way, like Pepé Le Pew. I showed him the article and he joked, "Aha, I need to start looking at more risqué magazines...for my heart health."

Sure, it's possible that looking at photos of women or

drinking a glass of wine every night would be good for your health, but I think you could replace those habits with something healthier, like taking a thirty-minute walk and drinking a glass of water. The fact of the matter is that alcohol is essentially a poison we take in small doses—it offers no real health benefits that you can't find elsewhere.

For the sake of making as much progress for yourself as possible, you need to assume that everything that isn't right in your life is your fault—this practice is called extreme ownership. That action alone is incredibly difficult for most people, because excuses are easy and relatively painless. "I was late to work because of traffic. I didn't go to the gym because I had a headache. I didn't move the dish into the dishwasher because it had to soak overnight. I took my clothes off and left them on the floor because"—the ridiculous excuses have no end. Owning up to our lack of discipline is an important step toward making our weaker areas in life stronger.

If we could exchange excuses for dollar bills, we'd all be millionaires by the time we're seventeen. Every day, we perform mental gymnastics to reason away laziness, apathy, and all the other ugly traits we don't want to acknowledge. We need to start catching our bad habits and shutting them down. For example, in my house, there's a joke between my wife and me about wearing our seat belts. If the seat-belt alarm goes off for one of us, the other looks over and asks, "Why don't you love our family?" The subtext is "If we get into a car accident, you might die because you are not wearing your seat belt. So, you must not love your family if you are not wearing a seat belt." The mindset is a little silly, but it creates an additional trigger to think—just for half a second—about something deeper than the possible inconvenience of clicking the belt, and that trigger works every time. You can use this mindset in making your bed, putting your dishes where they should go, or saying no to that one little drink. A little self-guilt is okay, especially when it is for a positive purpose.

My point is that you can begin to catch yourself, start addressing any bad habits, and take ownership of your actions. If it isn't working for you, don't chalk this up to being just the way you are. Of course, not everything is your fault. If you're tired after staying out late because your friend who drove decided to stay at the party two hours longer than planned, that's largely out of your control. Sometimes, other people are to blame, but if you focus on a mindset of extreme ownership, as opposed to looking to point out fault elsewhere, you'll find where you can be better. Everything else—the whole bar—moves up from there. You improve across the board by gaining a whole new level of commitment to yourself and those around you.

I adopted the idea of extreme ownership after reading a book of the same name by Jocko Willink and Leif Babin, two former Navy SEALs. The main argument in their book is that you should take full responsibility for your life. I couldn't relate to the military content of their stories, but their approaches and principles hit home. I read this book before I quit drinking, and it made me realize that I'm responsible for everything in my life because I control my attitude and my reactions to different situations. After this, naturally, the thought that I should probably give up drinking dawned on me. When being 100 percent in control of your life is a priority, alcohol becomes less of a priority.

PUT YOURSELF IN THE MINDSET TO QUIT

By adopting a mindset of extreme ownership and cutting out the bullsh*t with myself, there was no way for me to deny that the negatives of drinking far outweighed the positives. I simply couldn't justify consuming alcohol anymore. Someone might argue that I'd be losing the fun, parties, and social opportunities presented by alcohol, but those are still there in its absence. I didn't lose anything. I actually enjoy all of those situations even more, with far less of the anxiety that sometimes comes from social obligations.

After you spend time in the extreme-ownership space

with yourself and conduct some soul-searching, you'll raise your self-awareness and see the places you need to improve. Self-honesty clears doubt away and allows you to address your goals directly, whether that's waking up earlier, eating a certain way, or cutting out drinking. Personally, my newfound motivation helped me clean up my diet, start doing yoga, give up alcohol, and overall live a healthier life.

Part of figuring out why you're quitting is thinking about how this one goal ties in to your major life ambitions—your purpose. I had set out on Project Greatness for Adam, so to speak, and realized that the purpose most important to me is being a great father to my kids and great husband to my wife, and building the financial success that I couldn't have even dreamed of as a kid. I couldn't justify how alcohol squeezed into those goals. My motivation stemmed from my bad relationship with my alcoholic father and understanding how his behavior affected my brother and me. My biggest fear was ending up like him. While I never felt there was a danger of that actually happening, alcohol is a tricky vice. Nobody starts a relationship with drinking by planning for it to consume their life, yet it happens far too often or becomes a gateway into a lifestyle of regret.

Acknowledging that my relationship with my kids is a serious pillar of my motivation was, at the time, a pain point. Nothing makes you feel more like trash than being hungover when your kids want to play. A child doesn't know or care what being hungover means; they just know it's morning and they want to do things. I can remember the days when I would work all week, tear it up a bit on Friday night, and feel like crap on Saturday morning. When I wasn't awake and at my best on Saturday morning, my kids weren't getting their end of the deal, and to be honest, neither was I. When you think about alcohol that way, even when the drinking isn't overtly destructive, it's enough to bother most parents. When I think of the difference between getting up and accomplishing a lot of things, versus the feeling of lying in bed until noon, it motivates me to chase that good feeling and not chase the alcohol the night before.

My children will always be my number-one motivation to strive for greatness in every way. They're energetic little beacons of happiness, and at the end of the day, they're what keeps me grounded. Spending time with them, making improvements, and focusing on how to keep them happy is rewarding in and of itself. With the right mindset, you'll notice that things that might have seemed like a burden in the past now make you happy.

Another motivation of mine that everyone can—and should—share is health. Health is an easy goal to talk about with other people, and it can be your reason no matter what shape you're currently in. I think it is great how the health and fitness space has become cool and has motivated people over social media. I hope that trend continues to grow and change the way Americans view their health. For example, I'm in my late thirties and have stayed in good shape most of my life. I go to the gym regularly. As I mentioned before, I used to be a bodybuilder, so fitness has always been a huge, conscious part of my life. Still, no matter who you are, you can always be healthier. I want to achieve a higher level of health, especially as I get older, rather than feel like I'm slipping past my prime. Alcohol doesn't add anything positive to that bottom line.

You have control over many of the variables that contribute to your health: diet, exercise, smoking, drinking, hydration, sleep, etc. Getting older, obviously, is out of your control, but you can fight against its negative effects. One of my companies is a men's health clinic that helps with age management. Our clinic works with men who are interested in living a happier, healthier, more energetic lifestyle. People always laugh when I tell them I want to live to be one hundred and fifty years old, but it's true. I believe with technology and being proactive with one's health and lifestyle decisions, we are going to have many more people living well into their one-hundreds. I eat the occasional bowl of Lucky Charms, like any other person, but overall, long-term lifestyle changes come from creating good habits and eliminating bad habits, which is what the mindset to quit is all about.

Before I quit drinking, I consumed between three and six hundred calories almost every night in alcohol. When you stop to think about the calories in alcohol, it should be enough to convince you to seriously scale back. The heavier craft beers that are more popular now are in the range of two hundred to four hundred calories per beer. Can you imagine if you knocked back a few of those every day? That's almost ten thousand extra calories per week. If that is your lifestyle, you're going to have health issues from the calories, gluten, sugar, and, of course, the alcohol.

The time it takes to lose unwanted weight can be depressing, especially if you haven't put a stop to the bad habit that caused you to gain weight in the first place. Six hundred calories take about an hour on the treadmill to burn off. If you're drinking that much every night and not going to the gym, you're going to slide down that slope very quickly. I made it my goal to look better at age forty than I did at thirty-five, and being in better shape than you were five years ago is a goal that anyone can set, at any age. I will also say this. I have never, and I truthfully mean never, seen someone quit drinking and gain weight. They always lose unwanted weight and look 100 percent healthier and better!

Think about your purpose. This doesn't mean finding a date or buying a bigger house—purpose needs to be something real. It's the big-picture driver in your life, and it's what's going to keep you moving forward at the end of the day.

PREPARE YOURSELF FOR THE HARDEST PART OF QUITTING

It's easy to make a resolution, and also easy to break it. How many people do you know who make a resolution on New Year's Day, only to drop it two months, or even two days, later? It's much harder to make and keep a serious commitment like giving up alcohol. In some ways, making the decision to quit and finding your reason for doing it is the hardest part, but now that you know who you are and what you're going to do, there are still many challenges ahead.

Most likely, the part that was the hardest for me will be challenging for you as well: navigating social events and getting out of the social obligation to drink. You can't, and shouldn't, avoid social engagements, with the exception of absolute drink fests. The canoe trip I described in the previous chapter is a perfect example of the kind of social event you shouldn't avoid. There were people drinking, but there were others who had quit or simply didn't enjoy alcohol. Not drinking didn't make me stand out in that setting. On the other hand, a situation like my friends drinking beer in the garage might be something you should skip. That type of situation, where everyone is just standing around drinking beer, will be uncomfortable, because there's nothing else for you to do.

Unless you want a major eye-opener into how dumb alcohol can make people sound, you might also want to skip events like St. Patrick's Day or a bachelor party in your early days of quitting. Those events typically look very different through nondrinking eyes, and not in a good way.

Part of making your goal easier to keep is preparing yourself for social opposition. For example, when I started doing yoga, all my buddies said things like, "What's wrong with you? What are you doing? You're just there to check out women." I didn't let them get to me and kept doing my thing. After a while, some of the guys got curious and tried it, too. Guess who goes to yoga with me now? Almost all of them.

I roll into class with a bunch of meatheads and the yoga instructor grins at us because we're such an out-of-place sight, but yoga is the real judgment-free zone. My friends started doing yoga with me the same way most people pick up new habits or hobbies: they decided to try it once, realized it served them, and kept doing it. Be the pioneer of not drinking by being the first of your friends to make the decision to give up alcohol. Be proud of and confident in your decision, and I think you will see a few of your friends jump on the bandwagon with you, or at least abstain while they are with you. Not everyone can be as strong as you and embrace the infinite willpower it takes to quit alcohol. That's okay—focus on you! When it comes to drinking, you need to have confidence in your choice and believe you're doing the right thing. Friends might give you a hard time, but there's also a good chance they'll come to see that not drinking is working out well for you. They might even say, "Huh, that's cool. I'll do that, too."

Go into social situations knowing that your choice to quit might easily become the topic of conversation for the whole room. The subject might come up because someone wants to ridicule you, because they're harmlessly curious, or because there aren't enough other topics to talk about. How will you handle being put on the spot? If you mentally prepare ahead of time, hopefully it won't feel like being put on the spot at all. It's important to stay strong through the initial opposition or weirdness.

You need that internal drive to make it to the point where the bandwagon effect takes hold and you gain a group of supporters. When someone talks down to you about your decision, you're going to need to ask yourself, "Am I in control, or is my coworker/boss/family member/etc. in control?" The answer should always be you.

I've found the best way to deal with social situations is to embrace the fact that you've stopped drinking. As I mentioned earlier, think of people who go vegan, do CrossFit, or compete in Ironman triathlons—often, they're proud of what they're doing and aren't afraid to let you know. It is okay to talk about your new thing. If making a statement about yourself motivates you, by all means, do it. That said, don't turn into the person who says, "Drinking does this and that, and it's bad for you because..." Nobody likes a lecture about alcohol while they are trying to unwind with a few cold ones. You might create a negative space between you and your friends or add a negative hook to your new lifestyle by being pushy about *your* choice. Friends might worry you'll turn into that person. Show them you won't by being the person they know and love, just without a drink in your hand.

I'm reminded of discussing politics with my brother. We have vastly different views, but we have conversations about the issues. He is looking to run for local office, which

I think is great, but to win, he needs to understand both sides, not just that of his supporters. During one of our talks, I said to him, "If you want me to believe what you believe, don't tell me I'm wrong. Figure out why I hold my beliefs. With that information, find out how my beliefs and your beliefs might connect and argue from that angle." Giving up alcohol isn't as much of a hot-button topic as politics, but the same concept applies.

Being able to strategically discuss why you quit drinking alcohol is important. People are generally a bit self-centered and take too much personally. So, when you sit down with a friend you haven't seen in a while and they order a drink when you don't, prepare for them to feel a little uncomfortable. Then, when you tell them you don't drink anymore—that you gave up something they are literally doing right in front of you—some confused emotions can come from their side of the table.

People might voice strong opinions on the subject, and it's in your best interest to not be defensive or confrontational, but to understand where they're coming from. If you have a close friend who's always been neck and neck with you on drinking, your choice to quit will probably cause some major discomfort for them. They might think, "Why is he quitting? Does he think he's better than me? Do we not need each other as friends anymore?" It's best to make the decision and keep your response simple, short, and about you. "Yeah, I just decided one day to take a few months off from drinking and really never missed it or looked back. It's no big deal." That's it. Simple, truthful, and nondebatable.

It's comparable to ordering a salad for lunch and sitting down next to your friend who has a cheeseburger in front of them. They're going to look at your salad, look at their burger, and then look at you and think, "Oh, you're too good to eat a burger with me?" You can either believe that that's their problem and they need to deal with it, or you can try to make the situation as comfortable for them as possible, which may very well spark an interest in them to start the same journey. "Lately, I found when I have something lighter for lunch, I have a lot more energy for the rest of the day, but man, that burger looks good."

Not everyone wants to broadcast their life choices on a T-shirt, and some people will prefer to be more private about their decision. That's fine, too. You don't need to bring the subject up with people, but regardless, be ready to field questions. Eventually, you'll get to the point where you can say, "I'm me, and I don't drink. That's who I am. I don't care what other people think." Be stoked that you're doing something most people don't. It's a choice that should make you proud.

HOW TO HEAD OFF CHALLENGING FRIENDS

Unless your friends are terrible, most of them will support you. Seeing who supports you and who doesn't might even reveal who's a real friend and who you might want to cut. However, if someone gives you a hard time, it doesn't necessarily mean they're a bad friend. Their reaction might stem from something internal: thinking they should quit and feeling worse about their failure to do so when they see you not drinking. Give these people time, and if they're genuine friends, they'll come around.

Whatever you do, don't be the person who holds up two middle fingers to everybody drinking. If you create a safe space for your friends that doesn't make them feel threatened, you'll probably find that some want to join you. They may want to quit for Lent or New Year's or something else rather than give up alcohol forever, but they're still testing it out. If you were cool about quitting, they'll know they can call you up to talk about it or invite you out for Diet Cokes. I have a handful of friends who also decided to quit after seeing that I managed to keep my social life after giving up alcohol. I've found a lot of fulfillment in sharing the choice with them and knowing we can call each other up to say, "Hey, man. Want to hang out and not drink?" In turn, we show others that it's possible to hang out and have a good time without alcohol.

There are always one or two so-called friends who try to bring you down for your decision. Usually, it's because, on either a conscious or subconscious level, they know they could never make the same choice. These are individuals who aren't merely uncomfortable around you, but see you as their social competition. They're the ones who always try to one-up you, and if quitting drinking is a situation in which they can't beat you, they'll react badly. Their reaction may be trying to get you to drink, making fun of you, or calling you weak. You just need to stay strong.

Whether it's a friend, a family member, or a coworker, we all have someone like this in our lives. You may want to consider questioning the amount of time you spend with this person because they'll make your journey harder. When you are in their company, the most important thing for you to focus on is staying patient with them. Remind yourself that anyone who has a negative reaction to your decision is coming at you from a place of insecurity. If you let them growl and bark at you without lashing back, eventually they'll tone it down.

Some people will clash with your decision because they only see who you were in the past, instead of who you are now. For example, parents sometimes do this. When my wife and I first met, her parents constantly talked about her as a kid and never mentioned anything that she'd done after age ten. They've changed this behavior significantly since then, now that she's a wife and mother, but my point is that people who have known you for a long time can struggle to let the old you go.

Personally, in my twenties, people knew me as a promiscuous guy who liked to be the life of the party. There are people I haven't seen much or at all since my twenties who still think of me as the ladies' man party guy. No amount of them seeing me with my family and career successes is going to change their image of me completely, and to be honest, I don't care. You need to accept that some friends and family might not see that you're changing and will doubt your efforts. When they're giving you a hard time or pressuring you to "just have one drink with them," remind yourself that you're not the person they think you are anymore. You're in control of who you are now, and you will not waver on a major life choice to give someone else thirty minutes of false comfort. Stay relentless!

Lastly, you'll find that some people, primarily drinking friends, will fade away in the absence of alcohol. If there's something more between you, they'll stick around, but if there isn't, ask yourself, "Does it matter if I lose that person? Will I even miss them when they're gone?" If you weren't very close friends to begin with, it shouldn't bother you too much, but be aware that drifting can happen.

Giving up alcohol has helped my patience and empathy, but it has also made me more in tune with how others might perceive me. I want the people in my life to look at me and say, "You know, Adam, since you quit drinking, there's been no negatives." The alternative is them telling me, "Since you quit drinking, you're not any fun." I didn't want not drinking to change my personality, unless it was for the better.

FIND YOUR EXTERNAL EXCUSE

Once you've made your decision and identified your personal reason for quitting, the next step is developing an external excuse. As I discussed in the previous chapter, one strategy that made social situations much easier for me was having an easy excuse for not drinking. It's time for you to do the same.

Think of something that fits your life and will minimize discomfort for you and for other people. Here are a few ideas:

- It is/was my birthday, and I'm not drinking for thirty days afterward.
- I'm doing a thirty-day no-alcohol challenge.
- My wife is pregnant, and I'm not drinking in solidarity.
- I have a new baby at home and have to wake up at all hours of the night.

- I'm trying to lose weight.
- I've never gone a month without drinking since I turned twenty-one and want to try it.
- My buddy and I are seeing who can go longer without drinking.
- I gave up alcohol for Lent/the New Year/etc.
- I'm training for a marathon and have to wake up early to run.
- My relative/friend died from drinking.

The excuse has a dual purpose. One, it makes your friends comfortable with your decision because it makes sense to them. They understand the reason you've given them, and there isn't any cognitive dissonance to make them uneasy. To make them even more comfortable, try to replace drinking as a shared activity with something else. For example, ask if they want to split dessert. You'll fill the void of the alcohol bond and provide something to do together.

Two, your excuse convinces both you and your friends that you're making a big decision. By this I mean that if you can't keep your story straight about why you're quitting, you probably won't be able to commit to the change long-term. If you take your commitment, personal reason, and external excuse seriously, you will be able to stay unstoppable.

REPLACE ALCOHOL WITH ACTION

Once you've figured out how to manage difficult friends and family, the next step is to turn back to you. For me, that meant looking at the nonsocial side of my relationship with alcohol: my drinking at home. I knew I had to stop drinking a few glasses of Tito's every night and replace it with something new.

The easiest solution if you go home and drink every day is to fill the void with a new health initiative. For example, if you don't have a spouse or kids waiting for you at home, go to the gym. Skip the bar and skip drinking at home. After work, take your ass straight to the gym. It's the easiest swap you can make, and I predict two things will happen for you: (1) you'll never drink again, and (2) you'll never stop working out. You'll eat healthier, have more energy, and overall, feel better. Going to the gym is the low-hanging fruit of new habits.

I filled the void left behind by drinking at home with work. You need to assess your life and figure out where to devote your time. Here are a few ideas to consider:

- Exercising
- Focusing on work
- Starting a side hustle
- Taking on a new gig

- Applying for a different job
- Starting a website
- Writing a blog
- Reading a book a week
- Learning an instrument
- Taking an online class
- Volunteering your time
- Selling stuff on eBay

There are so many things that you can do to fill the space left by drinking, but it's important to choose one that you want to do every day. When I quit, I made a whole list of things I wanted to do and accomplish: grow my businesses, write a book, learn to play guitar, record a podcast, and do public speaking engagements.

Make a list for yourself and let it fill your free time. The worst thing you can do is to stop drinking and leave yourself to flounder for something to do. Like Indiana Jones, you need to swap the artifact with a bag of the same weight, otherwise you're going to find yourself trying to outrun a boulder.

When you don't have a plan, it's easy to just fall into the habit of watching television every night, and there's no less productive way to spend your time by sitting around drinking or watching television. The unhappiest, most unhealthy people I know live that way, and I think everyone who lives differently will agree that a slothful existence is the worst way to go through life.

If you adopt productive habits, you will find they have a snowball effect. You'll feel a sense of accomplishment, which feels good and motivates you to take more action, which leads to more accomplishment. You kick off a cycle of positive change in your life. Alcohol prevents you from taking action by bypassing genuine accomplishment and going straight to good feelings. You get the reward without any of the effort, but the reward isn't real, and when the alcohol wears off, you feel worse than you did before.

KEY TAKEAWAYS

In summary, here's what you need to do to successfully cut alcohol from your life:

- Be genuinely motivated to stop drinking. You don't need more than a desire to be healthier or more in control of your life, but there has to be a real source of motivation.
- Find your internal reason for quitting.
- Come up with your external excuse—the reason you tell other people that makes you and them feel comfortable.

- Plan a strategy for dealing with difficult or confrontational friends and family.
- Adopt a new habit to fill the void of alcohol. Choose something you want to do every day, and start a list of other activities you want to try.
- Own your new lifestyle.

CHAPTER SIX

NEW HABITS, NEW LIFE

Thinking back on those first thirty days of quitting, they were terrifying. I knew I wouldn't be able to get through it if I cheated and tried to cut down on my drinking—I had to stop completely. Based on my personality, I also knew quitting wasn't something I would just try out or do for a month before reverting. There was no undoing the realization that prompted me to quit in the first place: drinking didn't serve me. I had no reason to ever go back to my old ways.

"Forever" is a scary word, but I made my decision and declared it to the world. Knowing myself, that more than anything would keep me in line—I had told too many people to back out. I joke with my friends and family that I'm too dumb to quit. If I say I'm going to sell my company for $50 million, I'm going to put my head down and just go until it happens. However, because I give my goals 100 percent of my effort, I make sure to think them through before committing. Committing means devoting a huge amount of time and effort to the goal in question, and that isn't a decision to make lightly.

Time is valuable, and for most people, making a commitment to do something forever is probably the scariest part of giving up alcohol. Here's the thing to keep in mind: the longer you go without drinking, the easier it gets. The level of discipline you develop during those first thirty, sixty, and ninety days is going to spill over into other aspects of your life to great effect.

Personally, I may have smoked a couple cigarettes, drank too much Diet Coke, and ate a lot of ice cream, but it wasn't alcohol, and that made me proud. Knowing I had the discipline to turn down something that used to have a constant presence in my life kept me going through the process. I kept going and made it past the ninety-day mark. Making the choice every day to not drink was hard, but the positives outweighed the negatives, and the feeling of satisfaction was stronger than the sense that I was missing something. I realized that most of the fear and discomfort I felt was all in my head and had no bearing on how much I enjoyed life.

The further you go down this path, the more obstacles you overcome. The more you own the fact that you don't drink anymore, the happier and less fearful you'll be. You'll find you have plenty of good things going on that are completely independent of alcohol and, if you're like me, you'll find you actually enjoy social situations more.

For twenty years, I relied on alcohol to knock the edge off and help me feel more comfortable in social situations, but I've learned new ways to deal. I don't need alcohol anymore and am stronger for it, because there's nothing cool about relying on a substance to function. It's not impressive to be blackout drunk or hungover after a wedding. You're not achieving anything by drinking—anyone can get drunk—but waking up at 6 a.m. and going for a run? That's something many people can't or aren't willing to do.

There's good in the world—good music, good jokes, good experiences—that you don't even know about when you're drunk, but all these new things show up in your life when you have a clear enough head to look around. I'm at the point now where not drinking is simply part of my life and who I am. The process of quitting itself has changed me for the better. People tell me I look younger, and I wake up feeling great every morning. The positive feedback loop from not drinking has made me a better entrepreneur, a better partner, and a better parent. Never again will I have to explain to my son why I drank too much even though alcohol is bad for us. The hypocrisy isn't on the table anymore. Most importantly, I'm further than ever from being the kind of dad my father was to me.

My wife and I have been together for more than ten years now, and our relationship has never been better. She respects and supports my choice to not drink, and I do the same for her choice to continue drinking. We're both obsessed with self-improvement, support each other's hustle, and make an effort to communicate clearly, whereas for many couples, drinking exacerbates relationship problems. Alcohol leads to miscommunication, and by removing that risk factor, you reduce the chance of saying something that could be damaging to your relationship.

With time, social situations improved, too. My friends are all comfortable with my choice, and any awkwardness has long since faded away. Many see it as a legitimately cool choice and have given up alcohol themselves. The ones who still drink don't try to offer me alcohol anymore.

If we're at a bar, one of my buddies will just ask, "Diet Coke?"

"Yep."

"Okay."

My choice is no big deal, nor should it be. Fortunately, I think we as a society are trending toward being more accepting of going against the norm. Not drinking shouldn't be a weird choice any more than turning twenty-one should automatically mean you're required to drink.

The bottom line is if you want to be productive, experience growth in life, and reach your maximum potential as an entrepreneur or businessperson, you can't spend your time drinking. While you're out drinking, someone else has their head down working, and that person will win every time. I'm not saying you need to spend all your evenings working. The important part is that, when you are ready to work, you have a clear head. Time spent hungover is a complete waste, and if you run your own business, you need to be sharp 24/7.

My career improved at a rapid rate after I quit drinking, largely because I could work more efficiently, get more done, leave less on the table, take on new projects, do charity events and other gigs, and more. In effect, I had unlocked more hours in the day. Now my seven to ten, all the way through the next morning, wasn't muddied by drinking—I could use that time to work toward my goals.

When you face challenges head-on, they often open the door for more opportunities. A while back, I found a new distributer for my fitness supplement brand that was going to open my products up to a much larger consumer pool. Negotiations were going well until, fairly late in the game, the distributor realized they had a problem with one of our products and told us they had to drop the whole line.

I went into full doors-blown-off-the-hinges emergency mode trying to find a solution. Should we sell off all the product and eliminate it from the brand? Had this road-block happened six months earlier, I would have reached for a drink before trying to solve the problem and would likely have spent more time being pissed off than working toward a solution. Instead, I closed the door to my office and told myself, "I'm not leaving here until I figure this out."

I did solve that problem, and it worked out in a way that was better than the original plan. A new, bigger distributor agreed to pick up our brand, including the product the other company rejected, but it never would have happened if the problem hadn't come up in the first place. I would've had no reason to claw away at a better solution. My point is that problems often lead to opportunity if you're willing to work for it. Take whatever problems you face in quitting drinking and make them work to your advantage.

THE NINETY-DAY MARK

If you've committed, quit, learned to deal, and made it through the first days without alcohol, have another check-in with yourself at the ninety-day mark. Spend day ninety-one looking back on the previous three months and ask yourself the following questions:

- Have my relationships improved?
- Has my career or business path improved?
- Am I healthier?
- Do I have more energy and focus?
- Do I still enjoy social events with my friends?
- Have people supported my choice?
- Am I more confident?

At ninety days, I was more successful than I'd ever been before, and I'm willing to bet that when you reach that milestone, you'll know quitting was the right choice, too.

CONCLUSION

LOOKING TO THE FUTURE

I quit drinking out of a desire to improve myself, but also out of fear. Fear that if I didn't quit then, alcohol could become a problem. Whether that problem was a DUI, a strained relationship with my kids, or never achieving my life goals, these were outcomes I was unwilling to risk. There were still so many things I wanted to accomplish, and I realized I had wasted a lot of time at happy hours and sleeping through hangovers.

Now that I'm living an alcohol-free life, I can say without ego that I feel unstoppable. Not smarter, better, or faster—unstoppable. Alcohol was the one thing within my control that could sink the whole ship, and with it gone, I have a clear mind. I make better decisions, can pursue my goals with nothing getting in the way of my drive, and have earned additional respect from those around me.

The confidence that comes out of freeing yourself from alcohol is what's going to kick your life into the next gear more than anything else. I have seen so many people live a stagnant life full of mediocrity, accepting less than they are capable of and deserve. At some point in their lives, most of those people have had a bad relationship with alcohol. That bad relationship, whether from a dependency standpoint or serving as a social enemy, holds them back.

If you're a regular drinker and wish you had a better career, a happier love life, and a healthier body, quitting drinking will help fulfill those areas. I am on the other side and can tell you it's a better place for everyone. No matter what you're doing, when people notice your hard work is paying off and compliment you on it, you're going to feel great. If you drink regularly now, I guarantee people will notice you seem sharper after you quit, because you will be. To me, that's one of the greatest wins you can accomplish with any lifestyle change.

You'll be the best you've ever been, which isn't the same as saying you're better than other people. The only person you're competing with is your past self. You won't be better than your old drinking pals; you'll be a better friend to them. Better to your spouse, better to your kids, better to your family, better to strangers—better to everyone. Above all, better to yourself. You only get one chance at this beautiful life, and if you think removing alcohol can be a positive, I hope I have helped you find the strength to take the leap, because you can do it.

ABOUT THE
AUTHOR

ADAM LAMB is cofounder and CEO of SizeSlim
Supplements, a sports nutrition company, and cofounder
of an elite men's health clinic focused on lifestyle opti-
mization. A health enthusiast, entrepreneur, and devoted
family man, Adam took the same drive that enabled him
to become a competitive bodybuilder and to successfully
run two companies and channeled it into his commitment
to quit drinking on his quest to a "next-level" lifestyle.

Printed in Great Britain
by Amazon